Cartoons and Caricatures
of Mark Twain in Context

Studies in American Literary Realism and Naturalism

Series Editor
Gary Scharnhorst

Editorial Board
Donna M. Campbell

John Crowley

Robert E. Fleming

Alan Gribben

Eric Haralson

Denise D. Knight

Joseph McElrath

George Monteiro

Brenda Murphy

James Nagel

Alice Hall Petry

Donald Pizer

Tom Quirk

Jeanne Campbell Reesman

Ken Roemer

CARTOONS
AND CARICATURES OF
MARK TWAIN
IN CONTEXT

Reformer and Social Critic, 1869–1910

**Leslie Diane Myrick
and Gary Scharnhorst**

The University of Alabama Press
Tuscaloosa

The University of Alabama Press
Tuscaloosa, Alabama 35487-0380
uapress.ua.edu

Copyright © 2024 by the University of Alabama Press
All rights reserved.

Inquiries about reproducing material from this work should be addressed to the University of Alabama Press.

Typeface: Minion Pro

Cover image: Leslie Ward [Spy], *Below the Mark*, *Vanity Fair*, 13 May 1908
Cover design: Sandy Turner Jr.

Cataloging-in-Publication data is available from the Library of Congress.

ISBN: 978-0-8173-2172-7 (cloth)
ISBN: 978-0-8173-6104-4 (paper)
E-ISBN: 978-0-8173-9470-7

For Martha, Joseph, Jasiah, Cole, and Catalina

Contents

Introduction	1
Mark Twain "on the War-Path," 1869	7
Mark Twain and Moving Day, 1880	9
Mark Twain and the Campaign for International Copyright, 1882–1907	12
Mark Twain and the Concord School of Philosophy, 1883	19
Mark Twain the Satirist, 1891	22
Mark Twain in Australia, 1895	25
The "New School" of American Humorists, 1895–96	27
Mark Twain and Language Reform, 1897–1907	30
Mark Twain the Internationalist, 1897–1909	38
Mark Twain the Anti-Imperialist, 1901–08	43
Mark Twain's Return to the United States in 1900	63
Mark Twain versus the Cabman, 1900	66
Mark Twain's Campaign against Tammany Hall, 1901	71
Mark Twain on Christian Science and Mary Baker Eddy, 1902–07	76
Mark Twain and Censorship, 1906–07	81
Mark Twain among the Plutocrats, 1906–08	84
The Man in the White Flannel Suit and Dress Reform, 1906–07	88
Obituary Cartoons, 1910	96
Afterword	99
Appendix: Biographical Sketches of the Artists	101
Notes	107
Bibliography	113
Index	115

Cartoons and Caricatures of Mark Twain in Context

Introduction

WITH HAIR LIKE a fright wig, a beak-like nose, and his ubiquitous pipe or cigar, Mark Twain was "an excellent model for the caricaturist," the humorist Willis Brooks Hawkins asserted in 1905.[1] Eight years earlier, Twain conceded to his friend Joseph Twichell that he had been urged to sue a newspaper for libel after it published a caricature of him, but he had "no such disposition." As he explained, "I like the picture. I would rather be picturesque than pretty any time."[2] In any event, he was the inadvertent beneficiary of a so-called "golden age" of illustration that began in the 1880s, when technological advances in printing enabled magazines and newspapers to feature not only wood- and steel-cuts but high-quality zinc engravings and photogravure. In fact, between 1864, when he was a young staff reporter for the San Francisco *Morning Call*, and his death in 1910, Mark Twain was the subject of some six hundred caricatures and cartoons, virtually all of them published in newspapers and magazines. In this volume we reproduce nearly eighty of these images focused on Twain's opinions on issues of public policy and reform in sections organized chronologically by topic. In addition, the volume includes contextual headnotes to the sections, discussions and annotations of many individual drawings, an afterword, and an appendix briefly sketching the lives of the illustrators whose drawings we include.

To be sure, some significant episodes in Mark Twain's career, including some of the most (in)famous, failed to attract the attention of caricaturists. For example, his "Whittier Birthday Speech" in December 1877, that tempest in a Boston teapot, was not spoofed in cartoons. Nor was Twain's contribution to the Shakespeare-Bacon authorship debate, *Is Shakespeare Dead?* (1909), the subject of mock illustration, though some reviewers certainly ridiculed it. Among other gaps in the record mostly or entirely overlooked by caricaturists: Twain's speaking tour in India and South Africa in 1896; his notorious support for the Boxer Rebellion in China at the turn of the century; his opposition to the use of "the water cure" or water torture during the Philippine-American War; his campaign against vivisection and for the suppression of noise, especially on the Fourth of July; and his disavowal of Maxim Gorky when the Russian visited the United States in 1906 in company with a woman allegedly not his wife.

Still, *Cartoons and Caricatures of Mark Twain in Context: Reformer and Social Critic, 1869–1910*, is a type of visual reception history broadly tracing Twain's changing contemporary reputation based upon pictorial depictions of him and chronicling the evolution of his public image from comic type or humorist to social satirist. This development is evident in a comparison of the first two images. In 1873 Charles S. Reinhart depicted Twain as a jester in cap and bells flanked by Thomas Nast and Wilkie Collins in the center of the bottom row of his caricatures of popular American lecturers (see figure 1).

Figure 1. Charles S. Reinhart, "The Lyceum Committeeman's Dream," *Harper's Weekly*, 15 November 1873, 1013.

Nearly twenty years later, during the New York City campaign of 1891, Tyler McWhorter portrayed Mark Twain—who had endorsed a reform candidate for mayor—astride the winged-horse Pegasus, bearing an oversized quill pen as a lance and pursuing the Tammany Hall tiger into the underbrush under the caption: "Now will the Tiger take to the Jungle?" The cartoon alludes to the mythological Greek hero Bellerophon chasing the Chimera, a fire-breathing monster with the head of a lion, the body of a goat, and the tail of a serpent (see figure 2).

Nevertheless, in her essay "Post-Mortem Appreciation" (1903), Gertrude Atherton lamented the failure of the public to fully appreciate Mark Twain. The "greatest man of letters this country has produced," she declared in the midst of the controversy over his anti-imperialism; he "has intellectual power of the first order" and "there are few subjects upon which he cannot write with more acumen and illumination than anyone now before the public."[3] A cartoon that accompanied Atherton's essay pictured Twain royally robed and crowned with a halo—a far cry from jester's motley (see figure 3).

Figure 2. Tyler McWhorter, "Now Will the Tiger Take to the Jungle?" *Des Moines Leader*, 18 October 1901, 1.

Figure 3. *Appleton's Booklovers*, 1 (March 1903), 239.

This visual reception history also challenges the critical commonplace that Mark Twain was a beloved humorist in the celebrity culture of the late-nineteenth and early-twentieth centuries. In fact, he was not universally celebrated or adored, especially by the many public figures he mocked. More to the point, most of the images we reproduce appeared after 1890 and especially after his sharp left turn to social satire in 1901, when Twain was increasingly known as a controversial critic of Christian Science, an anti-imperialist, and an advocate for copyright reform.

Mark Twain was an avid consumer of graphic humor—he not only subscribed to several comic dailies, weeklies, and monthlies but also persuaded several caricaturists to send him original artwork—portraits not only of himself but on other topics. In many cases, cartoonists sent their original sketches or clippings of the published cartoons without prodding in the same way admirers and literary friends sent association books. Twain's high estimation of comic weeklies can be gauged from early lists of complimentary copies he had his publishers send for review. In a letter to Elisha Bliss Jr., he asks that "very early copies" of *The Gilded Age* be sent not only to the usual suspects—literary editors of the major newspapers—but also to editors of *Punch*, *Fun*, London *Figaro*, and the *New York Daily Graphic*.[4] In a letter to editor David Croly of the *Daily Graphic* in March 1873 Twain exhibited an intimate familiarity with the comic papers that survived about as long as fireflies in New York in the 1860s and 1870s. The illustrated *Daily Graphic*, he assured Croly, "is a marvellous paper—& the strangest marvel is that it seems to keep on going, like a substantial reality, instead of flaming a moment & then fading out, like an enthusiast's distempered dream. Every day when the carrier leaves it at the door, I think that that one doubtless contains the obituary (illustrated), & that he will collect his money now & come no more; but it does not result so, & I am one who is not sorry. Indeed, the pictures grow finer & clearer & softer, which is a surprising thing, & must be as gratifying to you as it is to me, I should think. I hope you will be able to keep it going all the time." Twain conceded that he did not "care much about reading (unless it be some tranquillizing tract or other), but I do like to look at pictures."[5] Just as his sojourn in England in 1873–74 had opened his eyes to new comic expressions, in Germany in 1879–80 Mark Twain developed a fondness for such German-language humor magazines as *Ulk*.[6] In a letter to his Hartford neighbor Morgan Bulkeley in 1883 he apologized for his delay in returning a borrowed number of the *Fliegende Blätter*, a comic weekly issued in Munich.[7] Several months earlier Twain had ordered a subscription to the paper from his European publisher Bernhard Tauchnitz: "I should like to become a permanent subscriber to the *Fliegende Blätter*; & I would also like to buy ten or twelve of the back numbers—I mean ten or twelve of the last years' volumes, which contain twenty-six numbers each."[8] However, Twain apparently did not break into the German-language comic weeklies until he settled in Vienna in

1897, when he graced the pages of several comic papers, including *Wiener Luft*, *Der Floh*, and *Kikeriki*. As late as 1905 Twain ordered a subscription to another Munich comic weekly, *Simplicissimus*.⁹

From his correspondence and interviews we know that Mark Twain requested and received the originals of cartoons by Albert Scott Cox, Ragnvald Blix, and David Wilson. After Cox's so-called "chanticleer" caricature of him appeared in the *New York Times Magazine* in September 1906, for example, Mark Twain pronounced it "the best one that I have ever seen of myself,"¹⁰ whereupon Cox presented him with the original drawing and Twain framed it (see figure 4). Twain successfully wheedled a number of original pieces from important cartoonists, but he also received artwork and clippings unsolicited. The archives at the Mark Twain Papers at Berkeley and the Mark Twain House in Hartford contain original boards of cartoons by Frank Nankivell and F. T. Richards, apparently gifts from the artists. Fred E. Lewis, who drew for *Puck* and other humor magazines, sent the author a well-known caricature of Twain as Huck Finn as a token of the young cartoonist's appreciation. According to Albert Bigelow Paine, the portrait was one of Mark Twain's favorites and was always prominently displayed on his desk.¹¹ It was first published in Paine's official biography of the author.¹² However, a cartoonist's gift occasionally was not well-received. In a 1905 interview Mark Twain compared a gag cartoon sent to him by the artist H. T. Webster, apparently as a birthday gift, to the so-called "gorilla" studio photograph executed in 1893 by Napoleon Sarony, which he despised. "I should

Figure 4. Albert Scott Cox, *New York Times Magazine*, 2 September 1906, 6.

like to be drawn once," Twain insisted, "as I should look if I had been made right instead of carelessly. . . . The longing of my heart is a fairy portrait of myself; I want to be pretty; I want to eliminate facts and fill up the gap with charms."[13]

A note on the parameters of this study: we exclude realistic renderings of Twain's likeness, especially when they were based on photos. That is, we try to recognize the common (if often oversimplified) distinction between "character" and "caricatura" or realism and burlesque. In addition, we omit all but two drawings (figs. 5 and 18) that appear on the pages of Twain's fiction and travel books on the grounds they portray a character rather than the author and so were subject to his approval. Moreover, these illustrations are readily available in online editions of his writings. Instead, we reproduce caricatures and cartoons, visual texts, and cultural artifacts that have a satirical, topical purpose from papers around the world whatever their circulation. While Twain was a master manipulator of the popular media and an expert at brand management, he had no control over these images. As Louis J. Budd, the late dean of Mark Twain scholars, once remarked, "Twain studies needs a finding list of photographs, portraits, and cartoons of him."[14] This volume represents a first step toward the compilation of such an iconography. It complements Milton Meltzer's *Mark Twain Himself: A Pictorial Biography* (1960), a hodgepodge of illustrations with little annotation or critical narrative; Budd's *Our Mark Twain: The Making of His Public Personality* (1983) and Dennis Welland's *The Life and Times of Mark Twain* (1991), which trace the growth and evolution of Twain's reputation; and Geoffrey C. Ward, Dayton Duncan, and Ken Burns, *Mark Twain: An Illustrated Biography* (2001), a photographic companion to Burns's documentary film. These four volumes all touch on the topic of Twain caricatures; however, none of them focuses on it exclusively. Our project is wholly distinct, moreover, from Beverly R. David's *Mark Twain and His Illustrators* (1986, 2001), a study of the art in his books and other publications.

We gratefully acknowledge the assistance of Robert Hirst, director of the Mark Twain Project at the University of California, Berkeley; Drita Choy of Zimmerman Library at the University of New Mexico; and Kathleen Galvin of the Center for Mark Twain Studies at Elmira College, who granted us access to the files Budd donated to the Center.

1
Mark Twain "on the War-Path," 1869

MARK TWAIN WAS a nascent social satirist from the beginning of his career, though the earliest targets of his satire were often benign. He was infatuated with the illustrations for *The Innocents Abroad* (1869), for example, not only because they were drawn by a gifted artist, True Williams, but because many of them pointed to a moral. "I like the pictures (for the book) ever so much," he wrote Olivia Langdon Clemens in March 1869. "Only a dozen or two of them are finished, but they are very artistically engraved. . . . They were drawn by a young artist of considerable talent. . . . There is one of me 'on the war-path,' which is *good*" (see figure 5).[1]

Figure 5. True W. Williams, "Return in War-Paint," *The Innocents Abroad* (Hartford: American Publishing Co., 1869), 124.

This caricature, which appeared in the prospectus carried door-to-door by sales agents, was later published in chapter 13 of *The Innocents Abroad* under the title "Return in War-Paint" to illustrate this passage of text: "The guides deceive and defraud every American who goes to Paris for the first time and sees its sights alone or in company with others as little experienced as himself. I shall visit Paris again someday, and then let the guides beware! I shall go in my war-paint—and I shall carry my tomahawk along."[2] Unfortunately, True Williams's career was cut short by his alcoholism. After Williams illustrated *The Adventures of Tom Sawyer* (1875), Twain wrote his friend W. D. Howells: "Poor devil, what a genius he has, & how he does murder it with rum. He takes a book of mine, & without suggestion from anybody builds no end of pictures just from his reading of it."[3]

2

Mark Twain and Moving Day, 1880

THE EDITORIAL CARTOONS featuring Mark Twain in the 1860s and 1870s had little to do with his political activities. Around 1880, however, when he began to campaign for expanded international copyright protections, Twain became a newsworthy personality whose opinions were cited in the front section of daily papers as well as the *feuilleton* or entertainment section. As he told a reporter for the *New York World* in May 1879—in only his tenth known interview—"Where an American author is interested 10 cents' worth in compassing international copyright the American publisher is interested a hundred dollars' worth in blocking his project."[1] Thus the pioneering political caricaturist Frederick Burr Opper pictured him a year later in the New York comic weekly *Puck* in company with some leading newsmakers, including policy wonks, failed politicians, robber barons, and ambitious clergymen.

The annual Moving Day in New York between the colonial era and the end of the Second World War was traditionally May 1, when apartment leases expired and many renters moved to more affordable or attractive lodgings. On this day refuse carts filled the streets to haul abandoned items to the dump. *Puck* took the opportunity in 1880 to ridicule the political hacks they opposed, especially Tammany *apparatchiks* or associates of the corrupt administration of Ulysses S. Grant, who was running for a third presidential term. "We should not have so strong an objection to moving," the editors opined, "if we could but cart off to some secluded spot a few of our political and social demigods and nuisances. If Uncle Sam would back up his truck against the back door of Republican or Democratic conventions and pitchfork or shovel into the vehicle a large proportion of the animated rubbish that infest them, we should hail the first of May with paroxysms of delight." The nation "had eight years of a strong man without a high and worthy purpose, and we ought to know pretty well what his 'strength' meant," that is, a "stench in the nostrils of decency."[2] In the rogues' gallery drawn by Frederick Burr Opper, Uncle Sam and Puck lead a band/garbage wagon filled with politicians, businessmen, assorted misfits, humbugs, and lyceum celebrities to the Dumping Ground: toward the upper left corner, a charwoman emptying stove ashes; Anthony Comstock, secretary of the New York Society for Suppression of Vice; Mark Twain, identified here as a supporter of Grant after famously toasting him at the Banquet of the Army of the Tennessee in Chicago in November 1879; and railroad magnate Jay Gould, who embraces Twain and who had supported Tammany candidates for years (see figure 6). Among the other caricatures: California labor leader Denis Kearney, well-known for his racism; railroad magnate W. H. Vanderbilt; inventor Thomas Edison; James G. Blaine, Speaker of the US House of Representatives during the Grant administration, who waves a bloody shirt, emblem

Figure 6. Frederick Burr Opper, "A Moving Day Fancy," *Puck*, 28 April 1880, back page.

of emotional efforts by post–Civil War politicians to exploit the Union dead for electoral gain; Roscoe Conkling, a stalwart Republican and US Senator from New York, who supported Grant for reelection in 1880; red-nosed former president U. S. Grant, holding a bottle of rye whiskey and wearing a crown; Samuel Tilden, former Democratic governor of New York and "hard money" Democratic nominee for president in 1876, who clutches a barrel marked with a dollar sign; the Reverend De Witt Talmage, "the jumping-jack of Brooklyn," preaching wildly from the cart pole; Ben "Beast" Butler, fondling a large spoon, a reference to his reputation for confiscating a set of silverware from a woman smuggling them out of a house during the Union occupation of New Orleans during the Civil War; Henry Ward Beecher, a Grant supporter and the most prominent minister in America, whose luster had been recently tarnished by a sex scandal; abolitionist lecturer turned actress Anna E. Dickinson, who had repented her support for Horace Greeley in the 1872 election; and Henry Bergh, founder of the American Society for the Prevention of Cruelty to Animals, whom *Puck* had dubbed the year before an "Apostle of the Police Club" and "Mr. Hum-Bug as a Humanitarian" for his defense of a policeman charged with battery.[3] Tammany strongman John Kelley, who had recently been denied the Democratic nomination to a US Senate seat from New York, has been thrown off the wagon and crouches on the ground to the left.

3

Mark Twain and the Campaign for International Copyright, 1882–1907

MARK TWAIN LONG labored under the misapprehension that his *nom de plume* was a kind of trademark protected by law, particularly after he won a suit for trademark infringement in New York state court against the publisher B. J. Such in 1873. When the sale of the authorized edition of *The Adventures of Tom Sawyer* (1876) in the United States was spoiled by the import of a pirated Canadian edition issued by Belford Brothers of Toronto, and especially after *A Tramp Abroad* (1880) was published without international copyright protections, Twain pressed the case for more rigorous universal safeguards for authors and resolved to secure imperial copyright for *The Prince and the Pauper* (1881) by residing in Canada when the novel was published in London.

His campaign for international copyright is illustrated in the next four illustrations. On November 25, 1881, Twain left Hartford for Montreal in order to establish the appearance of Canadian residency. It was his first prolonged trip north of the border. He celebrated the publication of *The Prince and the Pauper* by Chatto & Windus in London on December 1, and he returned to Hartford in mid-December. He received an unpleasant surprise less than a week later, however, when his application for imperial copyright on the novel was denied by the Canadian Department of Agriculture and Arts on the grounds that his two weeks in Canadian hotels constituted only an elective domicile. Had Mark Twain stated in the paperwork that he was a permanent resident of Canada—that is, if he had lied—the Ottawa government "would have been bound to take his assertion," the Washington, DC, *Critic* editorialized. The decision to deny Twain copyright in the British Commonwealth was "really extraordinary," according to the *Springfield Republican*, "for although everybody sees at once that such a sojourn is a mere fiction of residence, it has nevertheless repeatedly been accepted by the Dominion and copyrights granted accordingly."[1]

In the "most visible caricature" of Mark Twain of the period, according to Budd,[2] Thomas Nast satirized the denial of Twain's imperial copyright in a cartoon published a few weeks later in *Harper's Weekly*. In it, Twain stands before the Department of Agriculture ("truly rural-culture") office in Ottawa just over the northern border or "copy-right line" in Canada with a copy of *The Prince and the Pauper* under his arm. He is dressed like the character Bunthorne ("I'm an aesthetic sham!"), a satirical Oscar Wilde–type in the Gilbert and Sullivan

Mark Twain and the Campaign for International Copyright, 1882–1907

Figure 7. Thomas Nast, "Innocence Abroad (In Search of a Copyright),"
Harper's Weekly, 21 January 1882, 37.

comic opera *Patience*, soon to premiere on Broadway in New York (see figure 7). The medieval setting of Twain's novel apparently inspired Nast's portrayal of him in the pose of an aesthete. Teepees in the background are labeled "Ottawa," which referred, of course, not only to the Native tribe in the northeastern US and Ontario but to the capital of Canada. More to the point, Nast suggests the Canadian government equated books with farm produce, labeling the Minister charged with approving imperial copyright a "green grocer." At the entrance to the Department office hangs a sign: "Copy-rights granted here because authors are *so green* and never grow stale." The various vegetable baskets display ironic mottos: "Authors are small potatoes," "(dead) beets," "young turnips," "American squash some punkins." Atop a barrel of "lily white flour" rests a copy of Will Carleton's *Farm Ballads* (1873), which had been simultaneously copyrighted in the United States and British Commonwealth eight years earlier. A box of greens in the lower-right corner flies a pirate flag and the caption: "(We) cabbage (all we can from Yankees)."

As a member of the American Copyright League, founded in New York in 1883 and soon enlisting some seven hundred members, Mark Twain lobbied for new author protections. In an 1886 cartoon, Joseph Keppler emphasized the importance of the issue by both parodying Gilbert and Sullivan's comic opera *The Pirates of Penzance* (1879) and targeting European pirate publishers. A chorus of American, German, French, and English authors that includes Mark Twain at far left berate a pirate who stands on a law book, holding money bags, coins spilling from his pockets. Among the other writers pictured in the pitched battle are Bret Harte, Oliver Wendell Holmes, John Greenleaf Whittier, W. D. Howells, James Russell Lowell, Frank Stockton, George Washington Cable, Charles Dudley Warner, Emile Zola, Jules Verne, Robert Louis Stevenson, Wilkie Collins, Alfred Lord Tennyson, Robert Browning, Thomas Hardy, and Lewis Carroll (see figure 8). One of the receipts on the floor indicates that the publishing pirate had paid a mere nine cents for *Mark Twain's Joke Book*. The satirical libretto underscores the injustice of existing copyright laws:

> Chorus of British Authors: Behold the Pirate Publisher stand,
>   Stealing our brains for Yankee-land;
>   He's rude, uncultured, bold and free—
> The Pirate-Publisher: You bet your life: The Law—that's Me.
> Chorus of French Victims: He takes our novels and our plays,
>   And never a red centime he pays;
>   He is more Monarque than the Grand Louis—
> The P.P.: You bet your life: The Law—that's Me.
> Chorus of German and Other Sufferers:
>   The labors of our studious brains

All go to swell his sinful gains;
He ravages Norway and Germanee—
The P.P.: You bet your life: The Law—that's Me.
Chorus of Humble American Authors:
Though no one ever, in all this fuss,
Has thought of according rights to *us*—
Remember we're pillaged across the sea—
The P.P.: Who cares for *them*: The Law—that's Me.

Figure 8. Joseph Keppler, "The Pirate Publisher—An International Burlesque That Has Had the Longest Run on Record," *Puck*, 24 February 1886, 408–9.

In September 1902, nineteen conspirators, all former members of the Missouri House of Delegates, were convicted of municipal corruption in St. Louis. During the trial the prosecution revealed that each of the "boodlers" or corrupt local politicians had taken an oath "that in case I should reveal the fact that any person in this combine has received money, I hereby permit other members this combine to take the forfeit of my life and that my throat may be cut, my tongue torn out, and my body cast into the Mississippi River."[3] Mark Twain soon complained that they had plagiarized the blood oath Huck and Tom swear in chapter 10 of *The Adventures of Tom Sawyer* after witnessing Injun Joe's murder of Dr. Robinson; that is, they had violated his copyright of the novel (see figure 9).

For the rest of his life, Twain was an active proponent of extending authors' copyrights. He told a journalist who interviewed him in March 1904 that he never expected the members of the British Parliament or US Congress "to settle satisfactorily the intricate question of copyright" because the vast majority of the legislators did not understand the issues at stake. In "Concerning Copyright," the lead essay in the *North American Review* for January 1905, he noted that the copyright on Harriet Beecher Stowe's *Uncle Tom's Cabin* had expired years before she died and, as a result, while her publishers continued to profit on the book, Stowe's surviving heirs received nothing. That is, under the current law "the author's copyright expires just in time to permit his children to starve."[4] When he famously testified on December 7, 1906, before a joint congressional committee on behalf of a doomed law that would have granted copyright to authors, artists, and musicians for their lives plus fifty years, he predicted that, if such a measure passed, it would serve to feed "some starving author's children.... I like the fifty years' extension, because that benefits my two daughters."[5] The next month, he was caricatured in *Life* as he triumphantly sits on a barrel of "fine Havana" cigars and holds a scroll labeled "copyright" (see figure 10).

Figure 9. Alexander J. Van Leshout, "Mark Twain: 'Why, durn their boodlin' skins! This is plagiarism,'" *Chicago Inter Ocean*, 11 September 1902, 1.

Figure 10. "M. Twain-Clemens," *Life*, 31 January 1907, 161.

A new statute was finally adopted by Congress in 1909 that extended the period of copyright renewal from fourteen to twenty-eight years, thus permitting a work potentially to be copyrighted a total of fifty-six years. Twain thanked Champ Clark, a member of Congress from Missouri, House Minority Leader, and future US Speaker of the House, for supporting the legislation and assured him it was "the only sane, & clearly-defined, & just & righteous copyright law that has ever existed in the United States."[6]

4

Mark Twain and the Concord School of Philosophy, 1883

THE BRAINCHILD OF Bronson Alcott, a member of the Transcendentalist Club and the father of Louisa May Alcott, the Concord School of Philosophy served to perpetuate the philosophical idea(l)s of Emerson and Thoreau late into the nineteenth century. The school hosted several weeks of readings and lectures every summer between 1879 and 1888 in the Hillside Chapel, with a seating capacity of 140, situated behind Orchard House, the Alcott farmhouse near Concord. Emerson lectured twice at the school and attended occasional sessions until his death in spring 1882. But like Transcendentalism, its highflown rhetoric was also something of a popular laughingstock or the butt of satire. For example, Mark Twain had caricatured the fraudulent Emerson in his "Whittier Birthday Address" (1877) as "a seedy little bit of a chap" who routinely misquoted his own poetry.[1] After the story went around that the students of the Concord School had been challenged to a boxing match, a cartoon in *Life* depicted John L. Sullivan, the world heavyweight boxing champion, guest-lecturing at the school. The front-row audience includes (left to right) former US Secretary of State William M. Evarts as a crackbrained mad hatter; Oliver Wendell Holmes holding a copy of *Life*; an unidentified woman, perhaps the suffragist Susan B. Anthony; Ben Butler, the governor of Massachusetts, who had recently been refused the courtesy of an honorary LLD from Harvard College customarily awarded to holders of the office, here depicted as a yawning buffoon in cap and gown; and in the lower right corner, a dozing Mark Twain bored by the speechifying (see figure 11). The scene is wholly imaginary, of course: Sullivan, Holmes, Anthony, Butler, and Twain never attended a session of the school. All the celebrities in the front row are sleeping, yawning, or otherwise ignoring the speaker; Sullivan stands before the bust of a pirate rather than the bust of Plato that actually stood behind the speakers at the school; and portraits of criminals festoon the wall in the background. In all, the cartoon burlesques the facile optimism and faddish popularity of Concord as an intellectual center, and the school closed permanently five years after this cartoon appeared in *Life*.

Figure 11. Charles Kendrick, "The Concord School of Philosophy," *Life*, 9 August 1883, 66–67.

5

Mark Twain the Satirist, 1891

To illustrate his novel *A Connecticut Yankee in King Arthur's Court* (1889), Mark Twain hired the thirty-nine-year-old socialist Daniel Beard. By his own testimony, Beard had "never met Mr. Clemens until I started in to illustrate his book."[1] The author's directions to the artist were simple and to the point: "I have endeavored to put in all the coarseness & vulgarity into the Yankee in King Arthur's court that is necessary & rely upon you for all that refinement & delicacy of humor which your facile pen can depict." Twain urged Beard "to obey his own inspiration" because he wanted "his genius to be wholly unhampered."[2] Beard drew about four hundred pictures, over half of them reproduced in the novel, in seventy working days for which he was paid three thousand dollars, two thousand dollars more than he was promised.[3]

Twain began to read proof of *A Connecticut Yankee*, including the reproductions of Beard's sketches, in late August 1889. "I have examined the pictures a good many times," he advised the artist, "& my pleasure in them is as strong & fresh as ever. I do not know of any quality they lack. Grace, dignity, poetry, spirit, imagination, these enrich them and make them charming and beautiful; and wherever humor appears it is high and fine."[4] According to M. Thomas Inge, moreover, Beard expanded on Twain's topical satire by including "ideas not found in the text" in about one-fourth of the images.[5] Not that the novelist disapproved. Beard's illustrations constituted a complementary and parallel text to the novel and Twain commended them without stint. "Hold me under permanent obligations," he wrote Beard on November 11, a month before the release of the book. "What luck it was to find you! There are hundreds of artists who could illustrate any other book of mine, but there was only one who could illustrate this one. Yes, it was a fortunate hour that I went netting for lightning-bugs and caught a meteor. Live forever!"[6] Before the end of the year, Twain went so far as to declare that "to my mind the illustrations are better than the book—which is a good deal for me to say."[7] As late as 1905, in a speech to the Society of Illustrators in New York with Beard in the audience, he unequivocally praised the pictures in *A Connecticut Yankee*. "From the first page to the last" the book ridiculed "the trivialities, the servilities of our poor human race," he declared, and "the professions and the insolence of priestcraft and kingcraft—those creatures that make slaves of themselves and have not the manliness to shake it off. Beard put it all" into his sketches. "I meant it to be there. I put a lot of it there and Beard put the rest."[8]

In the frontispiece of *A Connecticut Yankee* Beard depicted the opening encounter of Hank Morgan and an attacking knight errant wielding "a prodigious spear." In counterpoint to the weapon, on a comic coat of arms in the lower left of the image, a helmet distinctly resembling a laughing frog surmounts a heraldic shield depicting three knights impaled on a giant quill pen. The motif of the victorious pen appears in two other illustrations at crucial points in the narrative. In the historiated initial for chapter 40, Hank Morgan's quill, dripping with ink/blood, severs the spine of knight-errantry (a pictorial reference to his having mowed down a band of knights in the previous episode with a pair of six-shooters). The image comes at a climax in the tale: "When I broke the back of knight-errantry that time, I no longer felt obliged to work in secret. So, the very next day I exposed my hidden schools, my mines, and my vast system of clandestine factories and workshops to an astonished world."[9] The "Final P.S. by M.T." in the novel contains an extra-textual illustration captioned "Hands Off! My Person is Sacred." It depicts Morgan as a composite figure, both a Yankee Doodle with a feather in his cap labeled "Macaroni" and a bearded, striped-trousered Uncle Sam astride a book entitled *Common Sense* (no doubt Thomas Paine's revolutionary treatise), who points the nib of a giant quill dripping with ink/blood at the belly of a portly monarch.[10] This image, the penultimate in the text, serves as Beard's paratextual summation of it.

In a cartoon widely syndicated two years after the novel's publication, Beard again explored the motif of the triumphant pen by depicting a pipe-smoking Twain shouldering a quill after skewering representatives of the three estates—a king who claimed the "sacred right to rule us," a holy man who asserted the "sacred right to think for us," and a businessman who reserved the "sacred right to rob us." A neatly folded American flag dangles from his pocket (see figure 12). The "pen mightier than the sword" motif runs through a total six of the cartoons in this volume. As in the Tyler McWhorter cartoon in the introduction (#2) and the Tim Murphy, Frank Wing, Francis Gould, and Gordon Ross cartoons below (#29, 35, 41, and 62), Beard depicts a quill as a weapon. Because quill pens required frequent sharpening with a pen-knife, they were often equated with spears or daggers. Similarly, Beard two years later twice caricatured not a knife running away with the spoon as in the nursery rhyme, but a quill pen running away with a sword in illustrating Twain's essay "Travelling with a Reformer" (1893).[11]

Figure 12. Dan Beard, "Mark Twain on His Travels," *Chicago Tribune*, 8 November 1891, 33; *Kansas City Times*, 8 November 1891, 8.

6

Mark Twain in Australia, 1895

Mark Twain, Olivia Clemens, and their daughter Clara Clemens sailed from Vancouver, BC, on August 23, 1895, to commence the Australasian leg of Twain's round-the-world speaking tour. During their well-publicized three-and-a-half months in Australia and New Zealand, Twain spoke publicly nearly fifty times in twenty-three cities and was routinely caricatured in the press. Unfortunately, he stumbled out of the blocks by committing a *faux pas* his first day in Australia. During an interview with the *Sydney Telegraph* on September 16, he hewed to the free trade line. "I don't profess to be learned in matters of this kind," he said, "but my instinct teaches me that protection is wrong." A few minutes later, shown a portrait of the eighty-year-old Sir Henry Parkes,

Figure 13. Livingston "Hop" Hopkins, Sydney *Bulletin*, 28 September 1895, 14.

the revered former premier of New South Wales, the so-called Father of Australian Federation, the "Nestor of Australia,"[1] and a champion of the protective tariff, Twain remarked that Parkes had "a truly splendid head" and that "it was hard to believe . . . he could make the bitter speeches . . . attributed to him."[2] As innocuous as these statements may seem in retrospect, Twain was immediately accused of interfering in Australian politics. The *Sydney Australian Star* damned him in its next issue for his "slanderous matter concerning Sir Henry Parkes." He "came to Australia to lecture" humorously on "morals," according to the paper, not to "discuss party politics, and if he had a tithe of the common sense he is credited with possessing he would have decided to leave the subject of party politics severely alone. Nor would he have been guilty of the meanness of making disparaging remarks, on hearsay, concerning Sir Henry Parkes, who is not nearly so black as he has been painted by Mark Twain." The *Australian Star* warned that his comments might cause hundreds of people "to keep away from the entertainments."[3] Luckily, Twain soon rectified his mistake with Parkes's help. The two men met two nights later at a dinner in Twain's honor at the Athenaeum Club in Sydney. Before a hundred members and guests, Edmund Barton, later the first prime minister of a federated Australia, proposed a toast to "Our Guest" which Parkes answered with "a magnificent reception."[4] A couple of days later, Twain told the *Sydney Times* that "your Sir Henry—he has the pull on me. I reverence that man's hair." He not only admired "the honey locks of the veteran" but "Sir Henry's oratory."[5] The American expatriate artist Livingston "Hop" Hopkins soon caricatured them chatting at the dinner. Parkes inquires, "What do you envy? My politics, my poems, or my brains?" to which Twain replies, "Alas! neither. 'Tis your hair consumes me with envy!" (see figure 13).

7

The "New School" of American Humorists, 1895–96

IN ANOTHER OPPER caricature, Mark Twain and the American literary comedian Bill Nye commiserate over a new school of American humor (see figure 14): public men of serious pursuits—politicians, economists, and journalists such as President William McKinley; Senator David B. Hill of New York; William "Coin" Harvey, advocate for the free coinage of silver and author of the fictionalized economic treatise *Coin's Financial School* (1894); and Whitelaw Reid, editor of the *New York Tribune* and one of Twain's *bêtes noires*—who were unintentionally funny in their public writings and speeches. Handkerchief in hand, Twain asks an exasperated Nye, "What in the name of Artemus Ward is going to come of us, if this thing keeps on?"

The artist F. T. Richards illustrated in the next cartoon a theme that often emerged in the pages of the comic magazine *Life*: "our over-advertised authors." The double-fold cartoon depicts a series of advertising posters attached to the outside of a traveling "literary side-show." A simian-faced copper leans against the canvas, casually twirling his baton, while a *Life* cherub works the door, offering a handful of tickets to a stray dog, the only apparent customer for this greatly discounted show. The sign reads: "Curiosities of American Literature, Admission 10 cents. Visitors Will Please Not Feed the Freaks." Mark Twain (center) is attired as Joan of Arc, a reference to the recent publication in book format of *Personal Recollections of Joan of Arc*, finally attributing the work to Twain the year after its anonymous serialization in *Harper's Monthly* (see figure 15).

The other writers caricatured are from top left: Frances Hodgson Burnett attired in the checked sporting gear of an English gentleman, a reference to the cross-dressing heroine of her best-selling novel *A Lady of Quality* (1896); John Kendrick Bangs, a recent candidate for mayor of Yonkers, dressed as "The Napoleon of Yonkers"; Brander Matthews, who had just published a pioneering study of American literature, in the garb of the New England–type Brother Jonathan; Amelia E. H. Barr parading "in her Bow of Orange Ribbon," a reference to her 1886 romance of that title; Francis Hopkinson Smith, the versatile author, painter, and engineer of the Race Rock Lighthouse, as "the Four-Armed Wonder" holding a small lighthouse, a quill pen, and a brush and palette; Mary E. Wilkins Freeman as "the Jolly Puritan" in a graveyard holding a small coffin, a visual allusion to the death of a child in her colonial-era novel *Pembroke* (1894);

Figure 14. Frederick Burr Opper, "The New School of American Humor," *Puck*, 10 July 1895, back page.

Figure 15. F. T. Richards, "Life's Literary Side-Show," *Life*, 28 May 1896, 434–35.

Elizabeth Stuart Phelps, author of *The Gates Ajar* (1868), holding a telescope to view "All the Wunders of the Heavens"; Julian Hawthorne, son of Nathaniel and Sophia, a gifted athlete and a recent immigrant to the West Indies, in the guise of "the Strong Man of Jamaica"; Ohio native and Harper's editor W. D. Howells as "Weary Waggles," a reference to an 1891 *Harper's Bazar* cartoon featuring an Ohio tramp; and the dashing, self-absorbed, Philadelphia-born war correspondent Richard Harding Davis depicted as "the Tattooed Ego Man from Philadelphia," ornamented with representations of his own face.

8

Mark Twain and Language Reform, 1897–1907

IN HIS ESSAY "The Awful German Language," originally published in an appendix to *A Tramp Abroad* (1880), Twain spoofed the arbitrary gendering of German nouns in which "fish is he, his scales are she, but a fishwife is neither," permitting such idioms as "the poor Fishwife, it is stuck fast in the Mire; it has dropped its Basket of Fishes" and "one Scale has even got into its Eye, and it cannot get her out." As for the difficulty of the language, he insisted that "a gifted person ought to learn English in thirty hours, French in thirty days, and German in thirty years." Separable verbs? Twain delivered a host of one-liners. "The German grammar is blistered all over with separable verbs," he whined, "and the wider the two portions of one of them are spread apart, the better the author of the crime is pleased with his performance." He joked that he knew a man who "would rather decline two drinks than one German verb."[1]

Twain echoed some of these points when he addressed a banquet or *Festkneipe* in his honor hosted by the Viennese Press Club on October 31, 1897. He delivered a speech in German, French, and English titled "Die Schrecken der deutchen Sprache" or "The Horrors of the German Language," a companion piece to "The Awful German Language." In its review of his comments, the *Neues Wiener Tageblatt* praised it with faint damns: Mark Twain "is a highly amiable and plain sort of a fellow, from whom nothing is so far as affectation and a desire to appear interesting."[2] The address was soon translated into English for publication in the United States.

In a cartoon that accompanied the text of the speech in the *New York Journal and Advertiser*, William Bengough pictured him as an oddball smoking an elongated porcelain pipe, dressed in sabots, nautical cap, black velvet smoking jacket, jacquard vest, and natty scarf (see figure 16). Similarly, Jimmy Swinnerton caricatured Twain a few months later in the *New York Evening Journal* as he declaims to a weeping Viennese audience from a book titled "German Verse by Mark Twain as Read by Himself." One person in the audience swigs from a bottle labeled "Vitriol" (see figure 17).

Mark Twain expressed mock scorn for translation in general in "The Awful German Language." Although he had acquired a rudimentary knowledge of "kitchen French" while on stopovers in Baton Rouge and New Orleans during his piloting career on the Mississippi River in the late 1850s, he purportedly

Figure 16. William Bengough, *New York Journal and Advertiser*, 21 November 1897, 33.

Figure 17. Jimmy Swinnerton, "Mark Twain's Oratorical Triumph in Austria's Capital," *New York Evening Journal*, 1 March 1898, 8.

disdained the tongue. As he facetiously complained in *The Innocents Abroad* while in France during the *Quaker City* excursion, "We never did succeed in making those idiots understand their own language."[3] Predictably, Twain was simultaneously amused and outraged when Marie-Thérèse Blanc (a.k.a. Th. Bentzon) translated "Jim Smiley and His Jumping Frog" (1865) from idiomatic English into faultless French and published the result in the July 15, 1872, issue of the *Revue des deux mondes*. "Got a French version of the Jumping Frog—fun is no name for it," he wrote Olivia when he read it. "I am going to translate it literally French construction & all, (apologizing in parenthesis where a word is too much for me) & publish it . . . as the grave effort of a man who does not know but what he is as good a French scholar as there is—& sign my name to it, without another word. It will be toothsome reading."[4]

He first published this travesty in translation, entitled "'The Jumping Frog' in English, then in French, then Clawed Back into a Civilized Language once more by Patient, Unremunerated Toil," in *Sketches New and Old* (1875). Whereas he had originally written, for example, "I don't see no p'ints about that frog that's any better'n any other frog," Madame Blanc wrote, "Je ne vois pas que cette grenouille ait mieux qu'aucune grenouille," which in Twain's retranslation becomes "I no saw not that that frog had nothing of better than each frog." "If that isn't grammar gone to seed," the author admitted, "then I count myself no judge."[5] The artist Frederick Strothmann illustrated a new edition of this 1875 story for Harper & Bros. in 1903 and portrayed a tormented Twain at his writing desk (see figure 18). Strothmann's drawings were so well-regarded by Harper & Bros. that he later illustrated Twain's *Extracts from Adam's Diary* (1904) and *Editorial Wild Oats* (1905).

In October 1903 the Clemens family sailed to Italy, in the hope Olivia Langdon Clemens would recover her health there, and settled in the Villa Reale di Quarto on a hillside overlooking Florence. Upon arriving, Mark Twain wrote a pair of satirical essays about Italian idiom reminiscent of "The Awful German Language." As he explained in one of them, "Italian Without a Master," he was not able to "speak the language; I am too old now to learn how, also too busy when I am busy, and too indolent when I am not." To be sure, the servants at the villa "talk Italian to me, I answer in English; I do not understand them, they do not understand me, consequently no harm is done, and everybody is satisfied. In order to be just and fair, I throw in an Italian word when I have one." Each morning, he claimed, he would learn a new word from the local newspaper. "I have to use it while it is fresh," he added, "for I find that Italian words do not keep in this climate. They fade toward night, and next morning they are gone. But it is no matter; I get a new one out of the paper before breakfast, and thrill the domestics with it while it lasts."[6] Albert Levering illustrated the essay with a sketch of Twain reading a paper while resting his feet on an English-Italian dictionary (see figure 19).

Though Mark Twain sometimes paid lip service to the topics of English language reform and reformed (a.k.a. "deformed" or phonetic) spelling, they were more often the butt of his humor. As early as the fall of 1899 he drafted an essay in support of "simplified spelling," though he conceded what was really needed was a simplified alphabet. "The heart of our trouble," he insisted, was a "foolish alphabet" that "doesn't know how to spell and can't be taught."[7] In January 1906, he proposed replacing "the measly word 'chauffeur,'" calqued or imported into English from French, with the south Asian term "mahout," which he had discovered while in India in 1896 (see figure 20). "Chauffeur is a good enough word when strictly confined to its modest and rightful place," he allowed, "but when we come to apply it to the admiral of the thunderous 'mobile or of the mighty elephant, we realize that it is inadequate. No, stoker is not the thing, chauffeur is not the thing, mahout is the thing—mahout is the word we need. Besides, there is only one way of saying mahout, whereas there are nine ways of saying chauffeur, and none of them right."[8] Homer McKee soon pictured Twain

Figure 18. Frederick Strothmann, "Mark Twain retranslating 'The Jumping Frog' from the French," *Harper's Weekly*, 5 December 1903, 1962.

Figure 19. Albert Levering, *Harper's Weekly*, 2 January 1904, 18.

Figure 20. Homer McKee, "I Christen Thee Mahout," *Indianapolis Star*, 14 January 1906, 1.

smashing a bottle over the head of a chauffeur whose goggles resemble a thief's mask and announcing, "I christen thee mahout."

In April 1906 Twain published his essay "Carnegie's Spelling Reform," in which he questioned the success of the Simplified Spelling Board financed by Andrew Carnegie,[9] and the following September he spoke at the annual banquet of the Associated Press at the Waldorf-Astoria in New York. In his speech, Twain attempted to persuade the press to adopt the bare-bones orthography proposed by the Board. The menu for the dinner featured several cartoons by "Hy" Mayer, one of which pictures Mark Twain dressed in a toddler's ruffed pajamas sitting on the floor playing with alphabet blocks with his winged wooden horse Pegasus in the background (see figure 21) and above a caption:

> His hobby was a hobby horse
> With wings of driven snow,
> And everywhere that Sammy went
> His hobby, too, would go.

Mayer executes here an ironic reversal of the heroic depiction of Pegasus as in the McWhorter cartoon reproduced in the introduction (#2).

Resplendent in a white flannel suit, Twain also spoke at the opening of the new Engineers' Clubhouse on Fortieth Street adjacent to Bryant Park and the New York Public Library the evening of December 9, 1907. Carnegie, who had

Figure 21. Henry "Hy" Mayer, *Washington Star*, 20 September 1906, 11.

financed its construction, was the guest of honor, and Twain exploited the opportunity to ridicule the steel baron's "pestiferous simplified spelling" proposal which, Twain facetiously asserted, like chastity could "be carried too far." The "real disease," Twain again alleged, was not the arbitrary spelling of difficult words but the "silly alphabet" that had been "invented by some drunken thief" and "doesn't have a real vowel in it, or a real consonant for that matter." He wondered aloud how Carnegie would "spell pterodactyl in private." If only "we had a sane, determinate alphabet, instead of a hospital of compound comingled cripples and eunuchs," he avowed, people "wouldn't have to learn to spell at all." Before finishing Twain blamed simplified spelling for "sunspots, the San Francisco earthquake, and the recent business depression."[10] The artist Oscar Cesare (see figure 22) afterward sketched a cosmopolitan Twain, full wine glass in hand, standing next to a laughing and tuxedoed Carnegie on the dais at the dinner while flicking cigar ashes onto the honoree's plate and sporting a suit of plain, double-breasted white-sack flannel, "the most remarkable suit seen in New York this season."[11]

Figure 22. Oscar Edward Cesare (1885–1948). Modified with permission of the Museum of the City of New York.

9

Mark Twain the Internationalist, 1897–1909

According to Greek legend, the philosopher Diogenes of Sinope carried a lantern while searching for an honest man. In chapter 32 of *The Innocents Abroad*, Mark Twain reminisced about his exploration of the Parthenon in Athens and observed, "I wished that old Diogenes, groping so patiently with his lantern, searching so zealously for one solitary honest man in all the world, might meander along and stumble on our party. I ought not to say it, may be, but still I suppose he would have put out his light" because he had found the man he sought.[1] In any case, Friedrich Graetz depicted Twain in 1897 on the cover of the Viennese humor magazine *Der Floh* (*The Flea*) as an American Diogenes blowing out his lantern, and the caricature foreshadows Twain's role early in the next century as an antagonist of military rulers like Presidents McKinley and Roosevelt, King Leopold II of Belgium, and Czar Nicholas II of Russia (see figure 23). Unfortunately, Graetz's optimism was misplaced. In a letter to the editor of *Harper's Weekly* in 1905, Twain joked that over the years Diogenes's task had become more difficult than ever.[2]

Figure 23. Friedrich Graetz, "Mark Twain in *Wien / Der amerikansche Diogenes*," *Der Floh*, 29, xlv (1897), cover.

In late 1895, the United States and the United Kingdom nearly went to war as the result of an escalating border dispute between Venezuela and British Guiana. Both countries claimed the territory of Guayana Esequiba, and President Grover Cleveland believed the claims of the British colony violated the terms of the Monroe Doctrine. While in Australia on his world speaking tour, Mark Twain worried about the prospect of hostilities, and he appealed for Anglo-Saxon unity in a dinner speech in Melbourne in October. "The Americans and the English and their great outflow in Canada and Australia are all one," he insisted. "Blood is thicker than water, and we are all related. If we do jaw and bawl at each other now and again, that is no matter at all. We do belong together, and we are parts of a great whole."[3] The crisis was eventually settled by arbitration, but Twain long remembered it. He concluded his remarks at the Authors Club dinner in London on June 12, 1899, with a pun that he claimed was eight days in the making: "Since England and America have been joined together in Kipling, may they not be severed in Twain."[4] Willis Hale Thorndike illustrated Uncle Sam, Kipling, and John Bull sitting side by side at the speech (see figure 24).

Figure 24. Willis Hale Thorndike, "Mark Twain—Since England and America Have Been Joined Together in Kipling [May They Not Be Severed in Twain]," *Boston Herald*, 15 June 1899, 3.

In an advertisement for a California business college, Beelzebub, accompanied by a black cat and a pair of bats, watches over the shoulder of a haunted Mark Twain as he writes at his desk (see figure 25). The scene is reminiscent of Twain's observation to Howells on September 22, 1889, after he completed *A Connecticut Yankee in King Arthur's Court*, a type of international novel: "Well, my book is written—let it go. But if it were only to write over again there wouldn't be so many things left out. They burn in me; and they keep multiplying; but now they can't ever be said. And besides, they would require a library—and a pen warmed-up in hell."[5] He had carefully tempered his criticisms of Great Britain so that the novel would not outrage Commonwealth readers. As he wrote Andrew Chatto, his British publisher, "I have taken laborious pains to so trim this book of offense that you might not lack the nerve to print it just as it stands."[6] Moreover, his comment to Howells echoes Nathaniel Hawthorne's remark forty years earlier that *The Scarlet Letter* (1850) was "positively a hell-fired story, into which I found it impossible to throw any cheering light."[7]

Figure 25. "Be Good and You Will Be Lonesome," *Stockton Record*, 18 November 1903, 4.

Mark Twain the Internationalist, 1897–1909 • 41

At the annual meeting of the Gridiron Club in Washington, DC, the evening of January 27, 1906, the guest of honor, President Theodore Roosevelt, was roasted for his Panama Canal policy. According to the *Washington Post* the next day, Mark Twain "was in his happiest vein" and spoke for nearly twenty minutes,[8] and Clifford K. Berryman accompanied the report in the paper with a drawing of some of the dignitaries who were present (see figure 26). Among those pictured are Roosevelt (center), Twain (upper right), Secretary of State Elihu Root (center right), Speaker of the House Joe Cannon (lower right), and Secretary of War William Howard Taft (lower left).

Figure 26. Clifford K. Berryman, "Among the Guests of the Gridiron Club," *Washington Post*, 28 January 1906, i, 6.

In a 1909 *Life* cartoon by Art Young (see figure 27), Mark Twain blows a puff of smoke while reclining on a rock and contemplating a rainbow while a "savage" is prostrate in the sand. The image illustrates the common-sense realism Twain practiced in his writing, epitomized by a credo found in chapter 43 of *A Tramp Abroad*: "We have not the reverent feeling for the rainbow that a savage has, because we know how it is made."[9]

Figure 27. Art Young, "Shots at Truth," *Life*, 14 January 1909, 73.

10

Mark Twain the Anti-Imperialist, 1901–08

DESPITE HIS WORLD travels, Mark Twain was a relatively late convert to the anti-imperialist cause. As he insisted in chapter 58 of *Following the Equator* (1897), written when he lived in England after circumnavigating the globe, "All the territorial possessions of all the political establishments in the earth—including America, of course—consist of pilferings from each other's wash. No tribe, howsoever insignificant, and no nation, howsoever mighty, occupies a foot of land that was not stolen."[1] He returned to the United States in October 1900 a confirmed and outspoken anticolonialist. As he conceded to the swarm of journalists who interviewed him at the dock, he had embarked on his round-the-world speaking tour in 1895 as "a red-hot imperialist" but returned "an anti-imperialist. I am opposed to having the eagle put its talons on any other land." In an explicit condemnation of US military adventurism in the Philippines, during an interview with eighteen reporters, printed the next day in dozens of newspapers around the country, he said:

> I have tried hard, and yet I cannot for the life of me comprehend how we got into that mess. Perhaps we could not have avoided it—perhaps it was inevitable that we should come to be fighting the natives—but I cannot understand it, and have never been able to get at the bottom of the origin of our antagonism to the natives. I thought we should act as their protector—not try to get them under our heel. We were to relieve them from tyranny to enable them to set up a government of their own, and we were to stand by and see that it got a fair trial. It was not to be a government according to our ideas, but a government that represented the feeling of the majority of the Filipinos, a government according to Filipino ideas. That would have been a worthy mission for the United States. But now—why, we have got into a mess, a quagmire from which each fresh step renders the difficulty of extrication immensely greater. I'm sure I wish I could see what we were getting out of it, and all it means to us as a nation.

When the war in the Philippines first started, he had acquiesced to the stated goal of the US government to "spread democracy through the region. I said to myself, Here are a people who have suffered for three centuries. We can make them as free as ourselves, give them a government and country of their own, put a miniature of the American Constitution afloat in the Pacific, start a brand-new republic to takes its place among the free nations of the world. It seemed a great task to which we addressed ourselves."[2]

But his views had changed dramatically while he was abroad. Twain concluded that the Treaty of Paris that formally ended the Spanish-American War did nothing to limit the authority of the friars who governed the country through a kind of clerical colonialism. He realized that "we do not intend to free but to subjugate the people of the Philippines. We have gone there to conquer, not to redeem. It should, it seems to me, be our pleasure and duty to let them deal with their own domestic questions in their own way." After the American fleet under the command of Admiral George Dewey defeated the Spanish navy at Manila Bay, according to Twain, Dewey should simply have sailed away. "He should have gone about his affairs elsewhere, and left the competent Filipino army to starve out the little Spanish garrison and send it home, and the Filipino citizens to set up the form of government they might prefer, and deal with the friars according to Filipino ideas of fairness and justice—ideas which have since been tested and found to be of as high an order as any that prevail in Europe or America."[3] Twain disputed the claim that Filipinos could not govern themselves. That is, given the civic corruption in New York and the "church-going negro burners" in the South—religious hypocrites on a grand scale—he argued that the Filipinos could govern themselves at least as well as Americans.[4] Moreover, he thought that the atrocities the United States performed during the war proved that the Filipinos were more civilized than the Americans. He condemned the water torture of Filipino insurgents—forcing water down their throats (a.k.a., in modern parlance, "waterboarding")—by US soldiers. Those who did it were, he said, "Christian butchers."[5] Twain even proposed a special flag for "the Philippine Province," as he called it: "we can have just our usual flag, with the white stripes painted black and the stars replaced by the skull and cross-bones."[6] The flag he proposed was a pirate flag.

The evening of December 12, 1900, less than two months after he returned to the United States after nine years abroad, Twain introduced Winston Spencer Churchill, the youngest member of the British Parliament and a veteran of the Boer War, to an American audience at the Waldorf-Astoria in New York. Twain took the chance to decry British prosecution of the War. Churchill was launching a US speaking tour, lecturing on the topic of South Africa under the management of Twain's former agent James B. Pond, moreover, so the mood in the hotel ballroom was convivial. "When Mr. Clemens arose and walked to the front of the platform," the *New York Sun* reported, "he got the reception of the star of the evening, the applause being long and hearty."[7] In his remarks, he bluntly expressed his own opinion on the subject at hand: "Mr. Churchill and I do not agree on the righteousness of the South African war," he avowed. But the two great nations were "kindred in language, in literature, and in civil liberty, and now that we are prosecuting an unjustifiable war in the Philippines, while Great Britain is doing the same in South Africa we are kindred in sin."[8] According to the *Sun*, "Clemens was cheered as much when he sat down as when he arose, although there were evidences of mystified celebration in some quarters of the room."[9] On his part, "Mr. Churchill seemed ill at ease when the chairman turned him over to his audience and traces of his nervousness remained throughout the evening."[10] Mark Twain had effectively upstaged one of the great orators of the twentieth century, as the *New York Evening Post* acknowledged the next day: "Mark Twain's reputation as a brief speaker on special occasions was considerably augmented by his remarks introducing Mr. Winston Churchill as a lecturer last evening. He drew the razor of his satire across several of the most flaunting and destructive humbugs of the age."[11]

In January 1901, Mark Twain assumed a vice presidency of the American Anti-Imperialist League, and in that office he lambasted the American missionaries in China in 1901, criticized the American military occupation of the Philippines in 1902, and condemned the murder and oppression of native Congolese by white Europeans in 1905. As Louis J. Budd remarks, "He stuck to the Anti-Imperialist League as long as it could afford stationery."[12] Twain was particularly incensed by the meddling of Western missionaries in Chinese affairs and their demands for financial compensation when the Boxers rebelled and reclaimed their territory. Twain vented his fury at William Scott Ament, the so-called "Father of Christian Endeavor in China," and his sponsor, the American Board of Commissioners for Foreign Missions, in "To the Person Sitting in Darkness," published in the *North American Review* in February 1901 to decidedly mixed reviews. W. A. Rogers caricatured Twain pelted by snowballs and preparing to retaliate with a clutch of his books at his feet, including *The Innocents Abroad*, *Following the Equator*, *Personal Recollections of Joan of Arc*, and on top a copy of the *North American Review*—this only three weeks after "To the Person Sitting in Darkness" appeared in the magazine (see figure 28).

As the next three cartoons illustrate, Mark Twain's essay stirred controversy and a wide variety of responses in the public press. In a caricature drawn for the New York *Bookman*, Tim Murphy depicts Twain as "a man of mark" defiantly standing on an oversized manuscript and wielding an enormous quill pen (see figure 29). Twain was portrayed in *Life* as a knight in shining armor or at least a quixotic crusader (see figure 30).

But other papers vigorously decried Twain's opposition to imperialism. For example, the *Minneapolis Tribune*, a pro-Republican, pro-protection, pro-imperialist paper, editorialized that a "great number" of readers "who dissent from [the essay's] radical views refuse to take it seriously and regard it as a piece of satire and exaggeration akin to the productions of the cartoonists."[13] Fittingly, ten days later an editorial cartoon by the staff cartoonist for the *Minneapolis*

Figure 28. W. A. Rogers, "Having the Time of His Life," *Harper's Weekly*, 23 February 1901, 214.

Figure 29. Tim Murphy, "A Man of Mark," *Bookman* 14 (September 1901): 9.

Figure 30. Louis Rhead, "The Brave Sir Mark," *Life*, 24 December 1903, 647.

Tribune hewed this editorial line by picturing Twain reading from a manuscript entitled "A Serious Essay on Anti-Expansion" while the Republican elephant laughs so hard a button pops off his vest (see figure 31).

Figure 31. Rowland C. Bowman, "The Best Joke Yet," *Minneapolis Tribune*, 20 March 1901, 1.

MARK TWAIN AND THE MISSIONARIES, 1901-02

Twain's indictment of religious and cultural imperialism in "To the Person Sitting in Darkness" predictably struck a nucleus of nerves and stirred controversy over the proper role of Christian missionaries in the Philippines and China that was mirrored in the editorial cartoons published at the time. Some missionary societies, in particular the Peking Missionary Association, insisted that he retract his criticisms and "gross libels."[14] Twain responded with a subsequent essay in the *North American Review* for April 1901 titled "To My Missionary Critics." As the *New York Tribune* remarked, the piece could be considered an apology only by someone "careless about the actual meaning of words."[15]

Ironically, the cartoonist for the *Minneapolis Journal* caricatured him as a savage cannibal—one of the rare cartoons that featured him as an ethnic or racial type—as he brandishes a manuscript as a weapon, heats his boiling pot by burning religious tracts, and a missionary hands him a "retraction" with the word "tract" emphasized (see figure 32). The cartoonist "Vet" Anderson drew the hirsute Twain with a grotesquely exaggerated mane writing at his desk beside a pile of books, two of them titled *Looting Through China* and *Don'ts for Missionaries* (see figure 33).

Figure 32. Charles Lewis "Bart" Bartholomew, "Can a Missionary Reach This Old Savage?" *Minneapolis Journal,* 23 March 1901, 1.

Figure 33. Jesse S. "Vet" Anderson, "Mark Twain in an Engrossing Moment," *New York Herald*, 23 February 1902, v, 5.

The Reverend Dr. Wayland Spaulding, president of the Congregational Clerical Union headquartered in New York, leveled perhaps the most demeaning insult, an *ad hominem* attack on Mark Twain's character in a speech at the Brooklyn Clerical Union on April 22, 1901. "All that can be said of Mr. Clemens," Spaulding averred, "is that he is a man of low birth and poor breeding."[16] The cartoonist Albert Reid soon depicted a hapless ministerial type from the New York Clerical Union hauling Mark Twain in a cart over ground pitted with such potholes as "caustic remarks" and "personalities" (see figure 34). Twain waited less than a week to reply to Spaulding at a meeting of the Brooklyn Clerical Union. A man of the cloth he declined to name "has just called me low born and ill bred," he noted. "I don't mind that so much. Shakespeare was low born, too; and there was Adam—I believe he was born out in the woods. But I'm glad the doctor didn't say it about Adam. When such a thing is said about the head of the family it hurts. Anyhow, I think I would prefer to be low born—in a republic—like the rest."[17]

Figure 34. Albert Reid, "Mark Twain and the New York Clerical Union," *Kansas City Journal*, 29 April 1901, 2.

William Scott Ament, one of the targets of "To the Person Sitting in Darkness," returned to the United States on furlough in April 1901 in order to defend his reputation and to raise more money for Chinese missions. The cartoonist Frank Wing imagined a confrontation between a diminutive "Dr. Ament," who demands an apology, and a bemused and quizzical Mark Twain, who again wields a quill labeled "satire" (see figure 35).

MARK TWAIN ON PHILIPPINE POLICY, 1901

Among the other targets of Twain's satire in "To the Person Sitting in Darkness" was US military policy in the Philippines. In an interview in 1895, Twain had urged "each man [to] kick his neighbor and receive a kick in return, until we have peace with courteousness."[18] The cartoonist Lorenzo W. Ford illustrated the essay in light of these comments. With a jokebook under his arm, Twain storms away from a limping Uncle Sam whose left leg is inscribed "Philippine Policy" (see figure 36).

Figure 35. Frank Wing, "Dr. Ament is undoubtedly courageous. He stood before the Boxers and addressed them, and now he has come back to America, where Mr. Clemens lives," *St. Paul Globe*, 22 September 1901, 1.

Figure 36. Lorenzo W. Ford, "The Kicking Joker," *Syracuse (N.Y.) Evening Herald*, 5 February 1901.

In one of the most nuanced contemporary cartoons featuring Mark Twain, Opper depicted President William McKinley ("Willie") as a child whining that "that Harrison boy and that Twain boy are scolding me!" Standing together in the foreground are a diminutive Mark Twain reading a passage from "To the Person Sitting in Darkness" and a diminutive former President Benjamin Harrison, who had published an anti-imperialist article, "Musing upon Current Topics," in the same issue of the *North American Review* as Twain's piece (see figure 37). The bloated patriarch "Papa" (the Trusts) sits in an easy chair and nonchalantly smokes a cigar as "Nursie" (McKinley's arch-defender, US Senator Mark Hanna of Ohio) barrels through the door to wipe Willie's tears. A caricature of Vice President Teddy Roosevelt, who had (in)famously endorsed a "big stick" US foreign policy the year before, hangs on the parlor wall.

Figure 37. Frederick Burr Opper, "Papa, Papa, that Harrison boy and that Twain boy are scolding me!" *San Francisco Examiner*, 12 February 1901, 14.

In its February 14, 1901, issue, the editors of *Life* rallied to Twain's side in the controversy and congratulated "our brother Mark" upon the publication of "To the Person Sitting in Darkness."[19] Two weeks later, the artist William H. Walker lampooned McKinley's Philippine policy by picturing a leonine, sober-faced Mark Twain posed like the winged lion in St. Mark's Square, Venice, scattering the imperialist triumvirate of Admiral George Dewey, the hero of the Battle of Manila Bay; President William McKinley flanked by a silver dollar; and Senator Mark Hanna, his suit adorned with dollar signs (see figure 38). Walker based his image of Twain on an iconic photo of the author taken by H. Walter Barnett for Falk Studios in Sydney, Australia, on September 16, 1895, and widely copied over the months in *Book Buyer*, *McClure's*, London *Idler*, and the London *Review of Reviews*.[20]

Figure 38. William H. Walker, "The American Lion of St. Mark's," *Life*, 28 February 1901, 166.

"THE CZAR'S SOLILOQUY," 1905–06

Czar Nicholas II of Russia prosecuted a war with Japan in 1904–05 in support of his territorial ambitions in Manchuria and Korea. However, the Russians suffered a series of humiliating military reversals, which in turn sparked popular protests of the czar's tyrannical rule. The Imperial Guard massacred a group of unarmed protesters near the Winter Palace in St. Petersburg on "Bloody Sunday," January 22, 1905, and only a week later Twain finished a draft of "The Czar's Soliloquy." In this imaginary disquisition, delivered while standing naked before a mirror, Czar Nicholas II acknowledges "there is no power without clothes." Without his royal robes he would be "as destitute of authority as any other naked person. Nobody could tell me from a parson, a barber, a dude. Then who is the real Emperor of Russia? My clothes." In modern parlance, he was nothing more than an empty suit. The original version of the sketch also included an admonition to Russian mothers to teach their children that as adults they should "knife a Romanoff wherever you find him; loyalty to these cobras is treason to the nation; be a patriot, not a prig—set the people free."[21] The piece appeared in the March issue of the *North American Review* and soon inspired an editorial cartoon by C. R. Macauley in the *New York World*. Macauley depicts Twain tipping the enthroned czar from his royal pedestal using a pen as a lever (see figure 39). The day the cartoon appeared, Albert Bigelow Paine showed him a clipping of it because it was "the kind of thing he was likely to enjoy."[22] His "angelfish" friend Gertrude Natkin planned to send him a copy until she learned he had "already seen it."[23]

A bizarre illustration for a 1906 article about Bloodgood Cutter, the "poet lariat" of the *Quaker City* voyage to Europe and the Holy Land in 1867, when Mark Twain claimed to have met Czar Alexander II, pictures an aged Twain warding the viewer away from Nicholas II (see figure 40). That is, the artist slipped a visual allusion to Twain's diatribe about the reigning czar into an essay entirely unrelated to him.

After the war ended with the negotiation of the Treaty of Portsmouth in August 1905, Twain criticized the deal for allowing the czar to survive the threat to his regime. As he declared when the Treaty was announced, "Russia was on the high road to emancipation from an insane and intolerable slavery. I was hoping there would be no peace until Russian liberty was safe. I think that this was a holy war in the best and noblest sense of that abused term, and that no war was ever charged with a higher mission. I think there can be no doubt that that mission is now defeated and Russia's chains revived—this time to stay. . . . One more battle would have abolished the waiting chains of billions upon billions of unborn Russians, and I wish it could have been fought. I hope I am mistaken, yet in all sincerity I believe that this peace is entitled to rank as the most conspicuous disaster in political history."[24] In Twain's opinion, the armistice was premature, a setback for the cause of Russian freedom and reform.

Figure 39. C. R. Macauley, "A Yankee in Czar Nicholas's Court," *Washington Star*, 15 April 1906, ii, 7.

Figure 40. *Washington Times*, 7 October 1906, magazine, 9.

"KING LEOPOLD'S SOLILOQUY," 1905–08

In interviews late in 1905, Mark Twain compared King Leopold II of Belgium, the proprietor and absolute ruler of the Congo Free State from 1885 until 1908, to a vampire who "sits at home and drinks blood" and to such killers as Nero, Caligula, Attila the Hun, Torquemada, and Genghis Khan.[25] Similarly, in his autobiographical dictation in 1906, Twain bewailed the atrocities of Leopold, a "bloody monster whose mate is not findable in human history anywhere," "probably the most intensely Christian monarch, except Alexander VI, that has escaped hell thus far." For over a generation Leopold exploited Congolese labor by "murder, mutilation, overwork, robbery, rapine."[26] Millions of Congolese died in the genocide, and Twain never wavered in his conviction that Leopold was a mass murderer. The "most effective and widely circulated piece of American propaganda in the cause of Congo reform," as Justin Kaplan describes it, was Twain's "King Leopold's Soliloquy,"[27] drafted on the same template as "The Czar's Soliloquy." Twain wrote the essay, the longest of his anti-imperialist writings, during the winter of 1904–05, and it was published in pamphlet form by the American branch of the Congo Reform Association in September 1905. In a Browningesque dramatic monologue, Leopold offers a pathetic defense of his barbaric behavior, all the while implicitly confessing to his crimes. He earns "millions of guineas a year" from his Congo enterprises and, he admits, "every shilling I get costs a rape, a mutilation, or a life." While his apologists once denied with impunity the claims that natives were brutalized under his rule, Leopold admits that "the incorruptible kodak" camera, by visually documenting physical mutilations, had become "a sore calamity to us" and "the most powerful enemy that has confronted us." Predictably, the published editions of the soliloquy featured photographs of amputees.[28] In a two-frame sequence, the British caricaturist Francis Carruthers Gould pictured Twain confronted by Leopold in the guise of a monstrous jumping frog that he then annihilates with a puncture from his writing quill (see figure 41). The artist "Dwig" Dwiggins drew Mark Twain dressed as an enthroned jester receiving homage from a bowing King Edward with a disconsolate King Leopold seated on the pedestal and chained to a ball labeled "Congo" (see figure 42).

Figure 41. Francis Carruthers Gould, "Mark Twain's Worst Dream," "There Was a Tremendous Explosion," *Perth (Australia) Western Mail*, 25 December 1907, 39.

IMPRESSIONS BY "DWIG"

Figure 42. Clare "Dwig" Dwiggins, "A Yankee in King Edward's Court," *Success* 10 (September 1907), 573.

Mark Twain; Pierre Mille, chairman of the French Congo League; and E. D. Morel, a journalist and founder of the Congo Reform Association in England, were crudely caricatured by Jean Villemot (Morel is to the right) in the radical leftist French weekly *l'Assiette au Beurre* as they appeal to the Public Conscience: "We will keep on throwing skulls at her feet until she will be forced to notice something is amiss" (see figure 43).

Twain's "King Leopold's Soliloquy" predictably sparked a backlash, particularly an official Belgian government response. The frontispiece to *An Answer to Mark Twain* (1907) pictures Twain and Morel as human-headed vipers coiling around a quill pen (see figure 44). The text of the pamphlet decries the "infamous libel against the Congo State under the title 'King Leopold's Soliloquy,'" an "ugly piece of work" that "met with no success in America" and protests that "no Belgian would take the trouble of discussing such filthy work." On the contrary, the Congo, a country twenty years earlier "steeped in the most abject barbary . . . today is born to civilization and progress."[29] The cartoon alludes to the infant Hercules's strangulation of the serpents sent to kill him by the goddess Hera and the presence of Satan in Eden.

Figure 43. Jean Villemot, "Public Conscience," *L'Assiette au Beurre*, 13 June 1908, 191.

Figure 44. Amédée Ernest Lynen, frontispiece to *An Answer to Mark Twain* (Brussels: Bulens Bros., 1907).

In a caricature published in both the *London Chronicle* and *Harper's Weekly* in the United States, the British artist David Wilson satirized both King Leopold's rule in the Congo and Mary Baker Eddy, the founder of the Church of Christ, Scientist (see figure 45). Mark Twain stands, arms crossed, with a wreath at his feet labeled "world-wide appreciation." A diminutive, veiled Eddy and a towering Leopold, his pockets bulging with "dividends" papers, commiserate in the background. Eddy holds a book entitled "Mark Twain on Christian Science" and Leopold a book entitled "Mark Twain on Congo Misrule." Eddy complains, "What he lacks, sir, is a sense of humour." Leopold replies, "Yes, Mrs. Eddy, Ma'am—and the power of appreciating disinterested efforts on behalf of suffering humanity." Twain had characterized both Eddy and King Leopold in comparable terms in *Christian Science* (1907) and "King Leopold's Soliloquy": as religious frauds and profiteers. Twain was so impressed with the drawing that he asked for the original while he was in England in the spring of 1907. A representative of the *Chronicle* presented it to him in his rooms at Brown's Hotel on July 1. "Old 'Mark' sat and conned it through his gold-rimmed spectacles with unfeigned delight," the journalist reported. "'Now that's bully,' Twain said, in his own simple-hearted way, 'that's mighty good! What I like about it is that it takes me just a bit seriously.'"[30]

Figure 45. David Wilson, "Mr. Clemens and the Marked Twain," *London Chronicle*, 20 June 1907, 3.

To illustrate a satirical essay by "Mr. Dooley," a.k.a. the American humorist Finley Peter Dunne, on "The Glorious Game of Football," a cartoonist for the McClure Syndicate mocked adults as though they were children at play (see figure 46). Notorious in Greek myth for castrating his father with a sickle and for swallowing his children to prevent one of them from usurping his rule, the Greek god Cronus oversees the scene like a puppeteer. To the left the railroad baron James J. ("Calamity Jim") Hill pulls a toy locomotive; King Leopold holds a bloody knife in one hand and an African effigy in the other; Mark Twain in a nightshirt fires a slingshot at Eddy, who sits with a copy of *Science and Health* on her lap and thumbs her nose at him; between them the financier, art collector, and philanthropist J. P. Morgan admires a Rembrandt painting ("Old Woman Paring Her Corns"); to the right the pacifist Andrew Carnegie rides a hobby horse featuring a dove of peace; and the oil magnate John D. Rockefeller spins a kerosene lantern labeled "[Stan]dard Oil." The scene is captioned, "'I think our young fellows take their games too serryously,' said Mr. Hennessy. 'I don't know about that, but I know us old fellows do,' said Mr. Dooley." Much as David Wilson in cartoon #45 compared Eddy and King Leopold to religious frauds, the McClure cartoonist places Eddy and Leopold in the company of robber barons.

Figure 46. Gordon Ross, "'I think our young fellows take their games too serryously,' said Mr. Hennessey. 'I don't know about that, but I know us old fellows do,' said Mr. Dooley," *Detroit Free Press*, 1 December 1907, iv, 3.

11

Mark Twain's Return to the United States in 1900

AT THE ANNUAL dinner of the Royal Literary Fund in London on May 2, 1900, shortly before his return to the United States, Mark Twain announced his mock-candidacy for president. "There could not be a broader platform than mine," he declared. "I am in favor of anything and everything—of temperance and intemperance, morality and qualified immorality, gold standard and free silver."[1] At the time the early boom of Admiral George Dewey for the Democratic nomination was evaporating. The *New York Press* editorialized that "the difference between Mark Twain and Dewey is that Mark was only joking."[2] In a cartoon by Ferdinand G. Long, a disgruntled Dewey stalks away as Twain throws his proverbial hat into the ring (see figure 47).

Figure 47. Ferdinand G. Long, "Dewey's Rival," *New York Evening World*, 4 May 1900, 6.

The Clemens family originally planned to return to America in June 1900 but postponed their departure when their daughter Jean suffered a bout of epilepsy, spending three months near London to allow her to continue her therapy. The family finally sailed from England and arrived in New York on October 14. On November 10, Mark Twain was welcomed home with a formal dinner hosted by the Lotos Club and attended by such Republican luminaries as former Speaker of the House Thomas B. Reed, Senator Chauncey Depew of New York, governor-elect of New York Benjamin B. Odell Jr., and Twain's friends Howells, Henry Huddleston Rogers, Thomas B. Aldrich, Booker T. Washington, and George Harvey. Twain improved the occasion by delivering a mock campaign speech and endorsing "free silver," or the monetization of silver, a perennial plank of the Democratic platform but anathema to Republicans. In his address, Twain declared that since he had been abroad the nation had "been nursing free silver. We have watched by its cradle, we have done our best to raise that child; but every time it seemed to be getting along nicely along came some pestiferous Republican and gave it the measles or something. I fear we shall never raise that child."[3] Two days later, the cartoonist C. R. Macauley depicted Twain bottle-feeding a silver dollar (see figure 48). Despite his career as a silver miner in Nevada and Twain's ironic advocacy of free silver, in truth he was an ardent supporter of "sound money" or the gold standard. In a dig at Theodore Roosevelt in the same Lotos Club talk, Twain mused that he "would have been a Rough Rider if I could have gone to war in an automobile."[4] Macauley also pictured Twain headed to the front in a horseless carriage.

Figure 48. C. R. Macauley, "We have done our best to nurse free silver," "I could have gone to the war in an automobile," *Philadelphia Inquirer*, 12 November 1900, 1.

To celebrate Mark Twain's return to the American strand, "Dwig" Dwiggins glossed on a jingle:

> I'm home says our dear old Mark Twain.
> And never shall leave it again!
>   Tho' they say I'm a li-on—
>   To be truthful, I'm tryin'—
> And I'll stay with my mite and my mane!

Dwiggins accompanied this ditty with a cartoon that depicted Mark Twain with an oversized head, prominent nose, unruly mustache, and attired in a high starched collar, Prince Albert jacket, and expensive shoes (see figure 49). He holds a jester's marotte with a ribbon on one end and a carved head on the other, and he points downward, presumably to indicate his intention to remain in the United States until he is consigned to the grave.

Figure 49. Clare "Dwig" Dwiggins, *Philadelphia Inquirer*, 14 September 1900, 16.

12

Mark Twain versus the Cabman, 1900

ON A TRIP to Chicago in April 1893, Mark Twain met an army major who contended that "every citizen of the republic ought to consider himself an unofficial policeman and keep unsalaried watch and ward over the laws and their execution."[1] Three years later he observed that "in London if you carry" a spat with a hack driver "into court the man that is entitled to win it will win it. In New York—but no one carries a cab case into court there. It is my impression that it is now more than thirty years since any one has carried a cab case into court there."[2] In October 1897, soon after settling in Vienna, Twain was overcharged by a cabman, whereupon he filed a grievance with the police and was assured "the driver would be arrested the following day." He "went home happy in the thought that he would have an opportunity for seeing justice dealt out in an Austrian police court. But the trial never came off."[3]

But on the evening of November 20, 1900, a month after the Clemens clan returned to the United States after years abroad, their maid Katy Leary was overcharged by the New York cabbie William Beck, who drove her from Grand Central Depot to the Clemens home at 14 West Tenth Street, a distance of thirty-two blocks or about a mile and a half. By city ordinance the fare should have been seventy-five cents. Instead, Leary said, the hack driver "took me all over New York. . . . Up and down he took me, all over Central Park"[4] before finally delivering her to her destination and demanding a fare of seven dollars or the equivalent in modern currency of about a hundred and thirty dollars. Mark Twain paid him a dollar, received an insult in return, and filed a formal complaint with the chief of the Bureau of Licenses for the city the next day, seeking the suspension of Beck's license. Overnight the controversy became a local *cause célèbre*, and "Dwig" Dwiggins redesigned his earlier cartoon to comment on it (see figure 50). Here the marotte is reversed, with ribbon and head on one end and a horsewhip on the other. Twain now hangs over a diminutive cabman to whom he points. The drawing is captioned with a Progressive slogan: "Mark Twain—to reform, begin at the bottom."

The public hearing on Twain's complaint became a media circus. "The room was just crowded," Leary remembered, with "lots and lots of reporters. They was even settin' up on the windows and on everything, these reporters was."[5] The *New York Evening World* reported that the hearing attracted "a throng which would have made a respectable sized crowd at a football game."[6] In the course of his testimony, Twain insisted he had filed the complaint not out of spite but

Figure 50. Clare "Dwig" Dwiggins, "Mark Twain—To Reform, Begin at the Bottom," *Philadelphia Inquirer*, 25 November 1900, 6.

"just as any citizen who is worthy of the name of citizen should do. He has no choice. He has a distinct duty. He is a nonclassified policeman, and every citizen is a policeman and it is his duty to assist the police and the magistracy in every way he can and give his time if necessary to help uphold the law."[7] In extenuation of his guilt, Beck explained that the competition was so stiff among the city carriage companies that the hack drivers "have to get square somehow.... We have to get all we can out of our fares." The owner of the cab company, Michael Byrne, similarly argued that cabbies deserved "special privileges," whereupon Twain "bristled up," his "eyes flashed," and he exclaimed, "The pirate can make that argument." The comment was greeted by loud laughter from the spectators and a reply from Byrne, who had misunderstood Twain's words: "You've been repeating parrot talk yourself."[8] The exchange was caricatured by Ferdinand G. Long in the *New York Evening World* (see figure 51).

Richard F. Outcault similarly pictured Twain in a two-paneled cartoon in the *New York Herald*, first as a uniformed policeman with a billy-club, then as a passenger inside a cab, the driver with a dagger in his belt waving a pistol and flying a skull and crossbones (see figure 52). The Chief of the Bureau of Licenses for the city commended Twain for performing his civic duty by filing his grievance and, as the plaintiff had requested, he suspended Beck's license.

Figure 51. Ferdinand G. Long, "Mark Twain, Reformer, Calls Cabman Pirate," *New York Evening World*, 22 November 1900, 1.

Figure 52. Richard F. Outcault, "Mark Twain's Idea of a New York Cab Man," *New York Herald*, 23 November 1900, 4.

Four months later, Mark Twain obliquely referred to the hullabaloo over the cabman's overcharge in a speech at a Lotos Club dinner. He joked that he once aspired to be the chief of police "not because I was particularly qualified, but because I was tired and wanted to rest. And I wanted Mr. Howells for First Deputy, not because he has any police ability, but because he's tired too. And I wanted Mr. Depew to be my Second Deputy, not because he's tired, but because he can do most anything well, and I could draw the salary."[9] Twain, Depew, and Howells were pictured as policemen in the next issue of the *New York World* (see figure 53).

Figure 53. "With Poets as Policemen, Mark Twain Would Purify City," *New York World*, 25 March 1901, 4.

But in the end Twain paid a price in reputation for his due diligence. The president of the Public Hack Owners and Drivers Association in New York publicly disparaged Twain for his actions: "He's a dead one. He's in the Potter's Field. I don't think much of a cheap man who will try to have an honest cabman's license revoked, all on account of a quarter. Mark Twain ain't got nothin' to do with us."[10] Still, the story of Beck's loss of his license had a happy ending if not a sequel. When Leary learned that the hack driver was the sole support of his widowed mother, she convinced Twain to intervene with the Bureau Chief to restore Beck's license. As a result, Beck "got a new job," according to Leary, and Twain even "paid him for the time he'd been idle since he was arrested."[11]

13

Mark Twain's Campaign against Tammany Hall, 1901

A SELF-DECLARED "MUGWUMP" or political independent since 1884, Mark Twain was outspoken in his criticism of Tammany Hall, the corrupt Democratic machine that dominated New York City politics for half a century. After his return to the United States in 1900 he routinely campaigned for reform candidates. "I'll vote for anything that opposes Tammany Hall," he insisted.[1] He endorsed the mayoral candidacy of the progressive Seth Low, president of Columbia University and the Fusion nominee, who was running against Edward M. Shepard, the pawn of Tammany, in the fall of 1901.

Twain's war on the political machine and civic corruption, like his anti-imperialism, spurred a backlash. The *Chicago Tribune*, for example, editorialized that "it was a serious error for Mark Twain to take off the cap and bells, which become him, and try to put on the mortarboard and gown."[2] Rowland C. Bowman, the staff cartoonist for the *Minneapolis Tribune*, a Republican organ, similarly depicted Twain, in a common comic motif, twisting the tail of a hybrid beast labeled "Politics" with the head of an elephant and the hind legs of a donkey. Twain has apparently escaped from the Joke Factory pictured in the background (see figure 54).

Figure 54. Rowland C. Bowman, "Better quit your foolin,' Mark, and go back and work at your trade," *Minneapolis Tribune*, 14 February 1901, 1.

At a rally for Low on October 29, 1901, before the Order of Acorns, an organization committed to civic reform, Twain decried the municipal fraud nurtured by the Tammany Hall machine and scorned its support for Shepard. As he declared, "A Tammany banana is easily detected. One end—the Shepard end—is sound and wholesome, but the other nine-tenths is rotten. Shepard believes he can purify the whole banana; but he can't. If we want decent government; here we must get rid of the whole banana. . . . The only way to cure this city of its grievous ills is to have a good doctor and I've got him right here and will now introduce him to you—Dr. Seth Low."[3] The *Brooklyn Eagle* reprinted Twain's entire speech on its front page the next day and in an editorial cartoon depicted Shepard as one end of a rotten "Tammany banana" bruised with "police corruption," "blackmail," "protected vice," "public plunder," "rake offs," and "crime" (see figure 55).

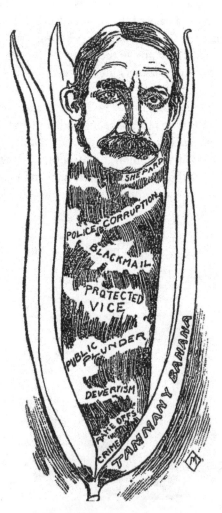

Figure 55. Claude Maybell, "The Tammany Banana," *Brooklyn Eagle*, 30 October 1901, 7.

The editorial cartoonist Thomas Nast began to represent Tammany Hall as a vicious tiger in the pages of *Harper's Weekly* in 1871. In the next three drawings, all printed during the New York mayoral campaign of 1901, Rudolph E. Leppert, "Bart" Bartholomew, and Tom Thurlby followed Nast's lead by portraying Tammany Hall as a tiger and Mark Twain as a tiger hunter. Leppert depicted Tammany on the run with Twain holding the tiger by the tail (see figure 56). Bartholomew caricatured Twain in working-class attire twisting the tail of the Tammany tiger and "belling the cat" (see figure 57). Thurlby pictured Twain confronting the Tammany tiger with a sheaf of one-liners as Shepard guffaws (see figure 58).

Figure 56. Rudolph E. Leppert, "Mark Twain Staying the Progress of the Tiger," *Anaconda Standard*, 3 November 1901, 22.

Figure 57. Charles Lewis "Bart" Bartholomew," "Kitty Does Not See the Joke," *Minneapolis Journal*, 18 October 1901, 2.22.

Figure 58. Tom Thurlby, "Will Mark Twain Attempt to Tickle Tammany to Death?" *St. Paul Globe*, 19 October 1901, 1.

On November 5, 1901, Low was elected mayor of New York with over 50 percent of the vote in a five-candidate race. Twain exulted in his notebook and privately claimed credit for the victory: "Who won it? Modesty almost forbids."[4] At a celebration in Times Square and a parade through lower Manhattan sponsored by the Acorns the day after the election, Twain predicted that, just as he had erroneously foretold the downfalls of the national Democratic party in 1876 and the national Republican party in 1884, "Tammany is dead and there is wailing in the land."[5] Unfortunately, his report of Tammany's death was greatly exaggerated. Low served in office only two years. Or as Louis J. Budd explains, "the antimachine coalition would crumble as usual before the next election."[6]

14

Mark Twain on Christian Science and Mary Baker Eddy, 1902–07

THE CHURCH OF Christ, Scientist, a spinoff from the New Thought movement of the mesmerist Phineas P. Quimby, a faith healer who once treated Mary Baker Eddy, was chartered in 1879. According to Christian Science doctrine, the physical world is an illusion and thus illness is nothing more than "false thinking" best treated through prayer. Eddy's following included friends and neighbors of the Clemenses, including Alice Hooker Day, with whom Olivia Clemens consulted about a possible treatment for their daughter Susy. In a note from Paris on February 4, 1894, she thanked Day for sending her a Christian Science pamphlet and assured her that "if I could only get hold of a fine woman in this thing I could certainly put Susy" in her care. "Just as soon as I am able to do so I shall have the treatment for myself and for Susy."[1] On his part, Mark Twain considered the sect a sort of organized fraud that resembled a political machine and operated like "a cash-&-piety" business. He ridiculed without remorse the "pudd'nheaded little Goddlemighty, Mrs. Eddy," and her holy writ, "her jackass 'Key' to the Scriptures."[2] In contrast to his deification of Joan of Arc, he demonized Eddy, "the queen of frauds & hypocrites."[3] To be sure, he was opposed not to Eddy's brand of "mental science" but to her profiteering. Her original sin, he thought, was plagiarism. Twain repeatedly asserted over the years that she had stolen her book *Science and Health* from Quimby and hired people to polish her prose, adding that in her own right she was "an ignorant twaddler. She can't write English; she can't write anything above nursery grade, she hasn't a vestige of reasoning power."[4]

Twain published a series of controversial essays on Christian Science between October 1899 and April 1903. His harsher arguments were, of course, often challenged by adherents to the faith, who answered him both privately and in print. A cartoonist for *Life* suggested he had been deluged with copies of *Science and Health* (see figure 59).

Ironically, in January 1903 Twain literally advertised in *Harper's Weekly* for a copy of Eddy's *Miscellaneous Writings*, claiming that no bookdealer would sell him one: "Mrs. Eddy's publishing agents having refused to sell me her book called 'Miscellaneous Writings,' to my great inconvenience, I have placed an order for this work with Messrs. Harper & Brothers, and shall hope that someone possessing an extra copy of it will be willing to sell it to them for me."[5] In a six-panel cartoon strip titled "The Man Who Corrupted Eddyville" and published in the next issue of *Harper's Weekly*, Albert Levering depicted Twain in a variety of disguises—in drag, as a hobo and a cowboy, as the Mississippi River pilot Horace Bixby, a Viennese aristocrat, and the Man Who Corrupted Hadleyburg—always attempting surreptitiously to buy a copy of Eddy's book (see figure 60).

At the invitation of the theatrical producer Daniel Frohman, president of the

Figure 59. Charles H. Ebert, "I have received two tons of 'Science and Health,'" *Life*, 24 July 1902, 76.

Figure 60. Albert Levering, "The Man Who Corrupted Eddyville," *Harper's Weekly*, 7 February 1903, 215.

Actors' Fund Fair, Mark Twain agreed to speak at the opening of a fundraiser on May 6, 1907, at the Metropolitan Opera House. He donated several inscribed copies of his books to be sold at auction, volunteered to autograph more copies of them at the Century Theatre Club booth during the Fair, and even authorized Frohman to "use my name and use it freely. Use it in any way you can think of that can help to raise money for that fund, which no right feeling and grateful human being can ever hear named without a leaping of the pulses and a warming of the heart. Forge it if you want to."[6] Then Genie Holtzmeyer Rosenfeld, president of the Century Theater Club, a devout Christian Scientist and wife of Broadway producer Sidney Rosenfeld, objected to Twain's role at the fair and, at a meeting of the club booth committee on April 30, demanded the return of the autographed books he had donated and the withdrawal of the invitation to him to appear in person at the Fair under the auspices of the club. She issued an ultimatum, threatening to resign if her demands were not met. Mrs. Rosenfeld "was very much affected at the committee meeting this morning," said a club member. "She told the members that her Jesus and Mrs. Mary Baker Eddy were dearer to her than any club or anything else in the world, and that she would rather give up anything than be associated with persons who publicly said about Mrs. Eddy such things as Mark Twain had said."[7]

The committee was gobsmacked. Its members adopted a formal resolution of apology to Mark Twain; and Edith Baker, the committee chair, hand-delivered a personal letter of apology to him. "Mrs. Rosenfeld is an Englishwoman," Baker wrote, "and does not understand that after the constitution and the emancipation proclamation, you are our biggest native document and our best beloved institution."[8] When Frohman learned about the bruhaha he was furious. He considered Twain's scheduled appearance at the fair a public relations coup. But he lit on a solution: he transferred Twain, with his consent, to the Players' Club booth. On his part, Twain accepted Baker's apology with grace and good humor.

Figure 61. Maurice Ketten, "A 'Tempest in a Teapot,'" *New York Evening World*, 3 May 1907, magazine, 1.

In a cartoon published in the *New York Evening World* on May 3, Maurice Ketten pictured Mark Twain, with an invitation from the Century Theatre Club in his pocket, holding a teacup beside a Century Theatre Club pot (see figure 61). Clouds of steam wafting upward are labeled "Christian Science muddle," "Mark Twain the man is nothing to me," "Resignation," "I can have no dealings with him," "Enemy of Christian Science," "She is an English woman," "Christian Science by Mark Twain," "Our biggest native document and our best beloved institution," "Religious grounds," "Mrs. Rosenfeld," "Mrs. Baker," "Actors Fund Fair," "The club is not a religious organization," "Apologies to Mark Twain," and "I will resign."

After this "tempest in a teapot," the fair was anticlimactic. Mark Twain was the "lion" of the fair, according to the New York correspondent of the *Cleveland Plain Dealer*. He was "surrounded by bevies of beautiful actresses."[9] He assiduously avoided the Century Theater Club booth, though some members "were seen to look wistfully at his white serge back, reflecting, probably, on what might have been."[10] The actress Ethel Barrymore remembered greeting him "at some big benefit at an opera house where there were booths. He was sitting in the book stall, signing things."[11] On May 10, the Century Theater Club voted to remove Genie Rosenfeld from its presidency.[12]

Twain's *Christian Science*, his last long book, partly based on earlier essays, was finally published by Harper & Bros. in February 1907. It contained an unflattering "character-portrait" of Eddy originally written in 1903 and epitomized by this statement: "Grasping, sordid, penurious, famishing for everything she sees—money, power, glory—vain, untruthful, jealous, despotic, arrogant, insolent, pitiless where thinkers and hypnotists are concerned, illiterate, shallow, incapable of reasoning outside of commercial lines, immeasurably selfish."[13] A year later, the artist Gordon Ross depicted Twain and Eddy in a faceoff on a spinning gyroscope (see figure 62). Eddy, whose dress is shaped like a carving knife, carries a copy of *Science and Health with Key to the Scriptures* ("Patent M.B.E.") represented as an oversized key and Twain, whose feet are bolted to the surface of the toy, is armed with a barbed quill and a bottle of ink.

Figure 62. Gordon Ross, "Mark and Mary / A Novel Gyroscopic Toy—Combines Science and Laughter," *New York Times*, 19 January 1908, 44.

15

Mark Twain and Censorship, 1906–07

IN AUGUST 1902 Mark Twain learned that the Denver Public Library had reignited the controversy over *Adventures of Huckleberry Finn* by purging the novel from its shelves on the grounds that it was "immoral and profane." Denver librarians defended their decision to ban the book because Huck "denounces the Sunday-school," "indulges in profanity," and "tells things more serious than fibs in order to wiggle expeditiously and safely out of embarrassing situations."[1] As Twain wrote the *Denver Post*, "Huck's morals" had "stood the strain in Denver and in every English, German and French speaking community in the world" for seventeen years.[2] The proscription of *Huck Finn* in Denver triggered a new round of banishments of the novel and other Twain books over the next few years from public libraries in Council Bluffs, Nebraska; Brooklyn, New York; and Des Moines, Manchester, and Sioux City, Iowa. On the whole, Twain was unperturbed. "I wrote *Tom Sawyer* and *Huckleberry Finn* for adults exclusively," he insisted to a Brooklyn librarian,

> and it always distresses me when I find that boys and girls have been allowed access to them. The mind that becomes soiled in youth can never again be washed clean; I know this by my own experience, and to this day I cherish an unappeasable bitterness against the unfaithful guardians of my young life, who not only permitted but compelled me to read an unexpurgated Bible through before I was 15 years old. None can do that and ever draw a clean sweet breath again this side of the grave.... If there is an unexpurgated Bible in the Children's Department, won't you please help ... remove Huck and Tom from that questionable companionship?[3]

Or as he reflected later, "When a Library expels a book of mine and leaves an unexpurgated Bible lying profusely around where people can get hold of it, the unconscious irony delights me."[4]

In response to the censorship, Irvin Alexander pictured a little boy consoled by the milquetoast Little Lord Fauntleroy ("you still have me") informing Huck Finn and Tom Sawyer that he can no longer play with them (see figure 63). Alexander mailed a copy of the cartoon to Twain, whose secretary Isabel Lyon wrote on his cover letter: "Likes the cartoon very much & thanks you for sending it."[5]

Figure 63. Irvin "I. Alex" Alexander, "Condemned," *Evansville Courier*, 30 March 1906, 1.

In April 1907, city controller Richard Joy of Detroit pronounced Twain's *A Double-Barreled Detective Story* "literary junk" unworthy of a place in the public library. In fact, he blasted most of the library commissioners' recent purchases, consisting of lovesick novels, poems, boy-hero stories, and other works of the same class and suggested that the money would be better spent on the "fresh air fund" that sent city children to the country for the summer.[6] A cartoonist for the *Chicago Daily News* depicted Twain entering a Detroit library and declaring "I wouldn't miss this for any amount" (see figure 64). Twain's book was restored to the shelves of the library the next month when Joy admitted "he had not read the book" before censoring it.[7]

Figure 64. *Chicago Daily News*, 26 April 1907, 9.

16

Mark Twain among the Plutocrats, 1906–07

During the final decade of his life Mark Twain routinely fraternized with plutocrats such as Henry Huddleston Rogers, vice president of the Standard Oil Company, and Andrew Carnegie, founder of the Carnegie Steel Company, while mostly turning a blind eye to the encroaching and corrosive influence of the trusts. Rogers, Twain's financial advisor, had snatched him from the jaws of ruin in the wake of the Panic of 1893. In 1906 J. Campbell Cory depicted Rogers's arm lifting Twain from a swamp of trouble (see figure 65). Mark Twain and Rogers were honored guests at the first annual Cartoonists' Beefsteak Supper held at Reisenweber's Café in New York the evening of April 18, 1908, an event caricatured by Fred Morgan in the *Philadelphia Inquirer*. The menu featured beefsteak and beer, consumed on liquor crates and soapboxes (see figure 66). When asked to give a speech, Rogers quipped that Twain "paid him for keeping silent."[1] The two men remained fast friends, an odd couple of sorts, until Rogers's death in 1909.

Figure 65. J. Campbell Cory, "He Lifted Mark Twain Out of Trouble," *New York World*, 14 January 1906, editorial section, 1.

Figure 66. Fred Morgan, "Mark and H. H. Rogers Getting a Square Meal," *Philadelphia Inquirer*, 20 April 1908, 2.

Mark Twain also had an ambivalent relationship with Carnegie. Both members of the American Anti-Imperialist Society, they addressed each other as "Saint Mark" and "Saint Andrew." Privately, however, Twain thought the steel baron sometimes amusing and at other times tiresome. He minced no words in assessing Carnegie's character in his autobiography: "I like him; I am ashamed of him; and it is a delight to me to be where he is if he has new material on which to work his vanities where they will show him off as with a limelight." He considered Carnegie's philanthropies, especially his funding of libraries that bore his name, merely an expression of his narcissism: "He has bought fame and paid cash for it; he has deliberately projected and planned out this fame for himself; he has arranged that his name shall be famous in the mouths of men for centuries to come."[2]

In a cartoon published in the *New York Press* a few days after Twain was awarded an honorary DLitt during ceremonies at Oxford University, Floyd Wilding Triggs depicted "Dr. Mark" in slippers and academic regalia, a reference to his notorious stroll down a London street in a bathrobe a few days earlier (see figure 67). "Chevalier Carnegie," who sports a Scottish cross around his neck (right) declares that his "gown looks like a bath robe." Meanwhile, "Prince Pierpont Morgan" (left), a renowned collector of medieval art and benefactor of the Metropolitan Museum of Art in New York, contemplates the royal crown and wonders how it "would look in the Metropolitan." Ironically, Morgan also purchased several of Twain's manuscripts, including the holograph of *Pudd'nhead Wilson*, now preserved in the Pierpont Morgan Library in New York.

Figure 67. Floyd Wilding Triggs, "Who's What," *New York Press*, 5 July 1907, 4.

Twain's transactional relationships with Morgan and John D. Rockefeller Jr., a devout Baptist who preached a gospel of hard work, charity, and abstinence, had little to do with his admiration for them and much with expedience. At the younger Rockefeller's invitation Mark Twain twice addressed his Bible class at the Fifth Avenue Baptist Church in New York and was elected an honorary member of the class.

At the laying of the cornerstone of the Pilgrim Memorial Monument in Provincetown, Massachusetts, on August 20, 1907, President Theodore Roosevelt accused a conspiracy of "certain malefactors of great wealth" of causing stress in the financial markets of the nation.[3] In a cartoon a year later, C. R. Macauley satirized Mark Twain as entertaining his clique of rich friends by reading from his autobiography. The major seated figures, rom left to right: Rogers, the railroad baron E. H. Harriman, Carnegie, Rockefeller, and Morgan (see figure 68).

Figure 68. C. R. Macauley, "The New Member / Malefactors of Great Wealth Club," *New York World*, 26 December 1908, 8.

17

The Man in the White Flannel Suit and Dress Reform, 1906–07

IN HER AUTOBIOGRAPHY, the novelist Kate Douglas Wiggin recalled that Mark Twain once complained about his normal wardrobe: "Think of the gloomy garb I have to walk the streets in at home, when my whole soul cries out for gold braid, yellow and scarlet sashes, jewels and a turban!"[1] In his autobiographical dictation for October 8, 1906, published in the *North American Review* for April 5, 1907, Twain confessed he "would like to dress in a loose and flowing costume made all of silks and velvets, resplendent with all the stunning dyes of the rainbow, and so would every sane man I have ever known; but none of us dares to venture it."[2] He was soon pictured in such flamboyant attire in the *New York Herald* (see figure 69). After "fine colors," he added in his autobiographical dictation, "I like plain white. One of my sorrows, when the summer ends, is that I must put off my cheery and comfortable white clothes and enter for the winter into the depressing captivity of the shapeless and degrading black ones," which reminded him of mourning weeds. Still, he never flouted sartorial convention by wearing white after Labor Day until the fall of 1906. On October 8, the same day he expressed the wish to dress in a "costume made all of silks and velvets," he likewise vowed "to get together courage enough to wear white clothes all through the winter" because it would "be a great satisfaction to me to show off."[3] At the most basic level, Twain sported a white suit in winter as a publicity stunt. "I don't like to be conspicuous," he told the artist James Montgomery Flagg, "but I *do* like to be the most noticeable person!"[4] He confessed to Earl Grey, the governor general of Canada, that his white garb was "premeditated— I got myself up so to attract attention."[5] To be sure, he repeatedly explained his motive in wearing white in other terms. He belonged "to the ancient and honorable society of perfection and purity," he proclaimed in December 1906. "I am the president, secretary, and treasurer. I am the only member" and indeed "I am the only person in the United States who is eligible."[6] "I wear white clothes both winter and summer," he declared in his autobiography, "because I prefer to be clean in the matter of raiment—clean in a dirty world; absolutely the only cleanly-clothed human being in all Christendom north of the Tropics."[7]

He debuted his new look on December 7, 1906, while testifying on behalf of new copyright protections at the Library of Congress. With the temperature in Washington, DC, hovering below freezing, Howells remembered, he arrived at

Figure 69. Wallace Morgan, "Mark Twain as an Oriental Prince," *New York Herald*, 28 April 1907, magazine, 1.

the hearing when Twain with a dramatic gesture "flung off his long loose overcoat and stood forth in white from his feet to the crown of his silvery head. It was a magnificent coup," and like Tom Sawyer "he dearly loved a coup."[8] Howells "laughed the buttons off his clothes," according to Twain, who wrote his daughter Jean from his room in the Willard Hotel that evening that he was the only person in the hearing room attired "in snow-white clothes. The others all wore black, & looked gloomy & funereal."[9]

Twain's appearance predictably made a splash in the press that rippled for months. The day after his testimony, Modest Stein depicted Twain in the *New York World* in brilliant white flannel that shimmers like a holy icon, to the horror of the dark-suited men behind him (see figure 70).

Figure 70. Modest Stein, "Mark Twain in That Cream-Colored Suit," *New York World*, 8 December 1906, 1.

George Sanglier, staff artist for the *St. Paul Pioneer Press*, pictured a glittering Twain on stage in a white suit with a price tag indicating it had been marked down from $10.00 to $9.98 (see figure 71). Mark Twain's immaculate white outfit soon inspired a jingle:

> The scribes of old were often cold,
> In shabby garb they wandered;
> I'd like to see Mark Twain's white suit
> Before he has it laundered.[10]

Figure 71. George Sanglier, "Mark Twain in Evening Dress Sketched from Telegraphic Description," *St. Paul Pioneer Press*, 17 February 1907, 1.

In fact, the caricatures of Mark Twain during this period often hung on the joke that, so long as he only wore white suits, he would need either to hire special laundry services or avoid travel to polluted industrial cities. Clifford K. Berryman, for example, depicted Twain in a white suit chased by Chinese launderers with a washtub, washboard, and ironing board (see figure 72). In a variation on the laundry joke, C. J. Taylor pictured Twain standing on a curb, smoking two cigars and wearing a white Spanish cape, as a bystander advises him: "You will spoil your white trousers if you cross here, Mark. Hold on, a mounted policeman will carry you over" the gutter (see figure 73).

In a three-panel cartoon strip, Archibald B. Chapin framed a visual joke about Twain visiting the steel town of Pittsburgh. From the right, Twain enters the city in pristine white clothing, passes through the soot and smoke from the mills, and exits to the left black in dirt and grime (see figure 74). Similarly, in a four-panel strip, Al Frueh, staff cartoonist for the *St. Louis Post-Dispatch*,

Figure 72. Clifford K. Berryman, "It's a poor fad that will attract no followers," *Washington Star*, 28 February 1907, 1.

Figure 73. C. J. Taylor, "An Easy Mark," *New York Herald*, 24 February 1907, 8.

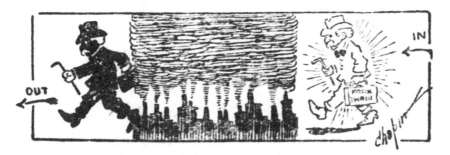

Figure 74. Archibald B. Chapin, "Passing Thro' Pittsburgh," *Topeka Herald*, 28 February 1907, 5.

pictures Twain arriving in the city to public acclaim, motoring by taxi to his hotel, and standing in the lobby soiled by the smoke (see figure 75).

During Mark Twain's trip to England to receive an honorary degree from Oxford University in the spring of 1907, he was introduced by George Smalley, the London correspondent of the *New York Tribune*, to the caricaturist Leslie Ward, a.k.a. "Spy" of *Vanity Fair*. Smalley promised Twain that Ward would "gently caricature and permanently immortalize you, if you will let him."[11] In his memoirs Ward reminisced about sketching Twain in his white suit: "The whole time I watched him he paced the room like a caged animal, smoking a very large calabash pipe and telling amusing stories. . . . He struck me as a very sensitive man, whose nervous pacings during my interview were the result of a highly strung temperament [see figure 76]. The only pacifying influence seemed to be his enormous pipe which he never ceased to smoke."[12]

Figure 75. Al Frueh, "If Mark Came to St. Louis," *St. Louis Post-Dispatch*, 15 March 1907, 12.

Figure 76. Leslie Ward [Spy], "Below the Mark," *Vanity Fair*, 13 May 1908, supplement.

18

Obituary Cartoons, 1910

THE EVENING OF April 21, 1910, with his daughter Clara and his physician Edward Quintard at his bedside, Mark Twain died of heart disease caused by years of excessive smoking. His final illness and death were, of course, topics of editorials and editorial cartoons across the country befitting the passing of a quintessential national hero. As M. Thomas Inge remarks, "Nearly every editorial cartoonist on a major newspaper commented on the loss through a cartoon memorializing the man or his work."[1] Louis J. Budd adds that "the patriotic motif" foregrounded in many of these drawings was "easy to evoke graphically."[2] The artists often featured a grieving Uncle Sam or Columbia. James J. Hruska in the Cedar Rapids, Iowa, *Gazette*, for example, pictured Uncle Sam, head in hand, holding a copy of the *Life of Mark Twain* (see figure 77). Rudolf Wetterau, staff artist for the *Nashville American*, portrayed Columbia in a classical white tunic presenting a bouquet of roses at the bier of Twain, who is draped by a large American flag (see figure 78). At his head are a pile of laurel crowns and a funereal torch that emits a large banner of smoke containing the titles of several of his works, including *Innocence* [sic] *Abroad*. Other artists, such as Clare Briggs in the *Chicago Tribune*, honored Mark Twain's memory by depicting a cluster of Twain's characters, usually Huck and Tom, in mourning (see figure 79).

Figure 77. James J. Hruska, "The End," *Cedar Rapids (Ia.) Gazette*, 22 April 1910, 1.

Figure 78. M. Rudolf Wetterau, "Columbia in Deepest Grief," *Nashville American*, 23 April 1910, 4.

Figure 79. Clare Briggs, *Chicago Tribune*, 22 April 1910, 1.

Afterword

Harold K. Bush Jr. opined in 2007 that Twain's likeness, whether photographed, drawn, or sculpted, was probably "the most frequently reproduced of any person in all of human history" when he died.[1] This volume is the first installment of the iconography that Twain scholars over the past couple of generations have hoped would be compiled. It also features facets of Twain's career often ignored or overlooked, such as his advocacy of language reform, dress reform, spelling reform, and free trade.

The images reproduced in this book should also prove useful as tools for teachers of Mark Twain's *A Connecticut Yankee in King Arthurs's Court* as well as teachers of his late short writings, especially "To the Person Sitting in Darkness," "The Czar's Soliloquy," and "King Leopold's Soliloquy."

Appendix:
Biographical Sketches of the Artists

Irvin Alexander (1873–1910) studied art in Chicago before drawing for the *Evansville Courier*.

Jesse S. "Vet" Anderson (1873–1966), nicknamed for his service in the Spanish-American War, contributed to the *Detroit Free Press* in 1899 and worked a short time for the *Chicago Journal* before joining the staffs of the *New York Herald* and the *New York World*.

Charles Lewis "Bart" Bartholomew (1869–1949) was a self-taught artist and pro-imperialist staff cartoonist for the *Minneapolis Journal* whose drawings were syndicated by the Scripps Editorial Alliance.

Dan Beard (1850–1941), educated at the Art Students' League in New York, illustrated several of Twain's books, including *A Connecticut Yankee in King Arthur's Court*.

William Bengough (1863–1932) was a Canadian-born illustrator who served as a special artist for *Harper's Monthly* in Vienna, where he covered the death of Elizabeth of Austria. He also sent back vivid illustrations from the battlefield during the Spanish-American War.

Clifford K. Berryman (1869–1949) worked for the *Washington Post* and *Evening Star*. Berryman received the Pulitzer Prize for Editorial Cartooning in 1944.

Rowland C. Bowman (1870–1903) contributed cartoons to the *Chicago Inter-Ocean* and *Minneapolis Times* before becoming a staff artist for the *Minneapolis Tribune* in 1897.

Clare Briggs (1875–1930) began his career as an artist for the *St. Louis Globe-Democrat* in 1896 and following a short stint at the *New York Journal* worked for the *Chicago Tribune* for nearly two decades.

Oscar Cesare (1883–1948) studied art in Paris before working for the *Chicago Tribune*. He also contributed to the *New York World*, *Sun*, and *Evening Post*.

Archibald B. Chapin (1875–1962) worked for the *Kansas City Star* until 1913.

John Campbell Cory (1867–1925) was an illustrator and cartoonist for the *New York Journal*, *New York World*, *Rocky Mountain News*, and *Denver Times*.

Albert Scott Cox (1863–1920) was a painter, illustrator, and caricaturist born in Massachusetts. He worked as an artist in Boston until around 1900, when he moved to New York. Cox contributed caricatures to the *New York Times*, *New York World*, and *Chicago Daily News*.

Clare "Dwig" Dwiggins (1874–1958) worked for the *St. Louis Post-Dispatch* and *Philadelphia Inquirer*. In 1905 he moved to New York and drew for the *New York Evening Journal* and the *New York World*.

Charles Henry Ebert (1873–1959) studied at the Art Academy in Cincinnati, the Art Students' League in New York, and the Académie Julian in Paris. He was a staff illustrator for *Life* and contributed to *Cosmopolitan*.

Lorenzo W. Ford (1866–1925) worked for the *Syracuse Herald* and later drew for the *New York Evening World*.

Al Frueh (1880–1968) worked for the *St. Louis Post-Dispatch* and the *New York World*.

Francis Carruthers Gould (1844–1925) contributed to *Truth*, the *Pall Mall Gazette*, and the *Westminster Gazette*.

Friedrich Graetz (1842–1912) studied art with Eduard van Steinle. In 1867 he moved to Vienna and began to draw for *Kikeriki* and *Der Floh*.

Livingston "Hop" Hopkins (1846–1927) began his career as a staff illustrator for the *Toledo Blade* and in 1870 moved to New York, where he freelanced for *Collier's Weekly*, *Chic*, *Judge*, and other papers. In 1882 he emigrated to Australia, where he worked with cartoonist Phil May.

James J. Hruska (1877–1945) was for many years the staff cartoonist for the Cedar Rapids, Iowa, *Gazette*.

Charles Kendrick (1841–1914) was born in London and emigrated to the United States in 1873 and worked for *Frank Leslie's Illustrated Newspaper*. He was the chief cartoonist for the short-lived but popular *Chic* comic weekly (1880–1881), published in New York. He also contributed to the *National Police Gazette*, *Harper's Weekly*, *Life*, and *Snap*.

Joseph Keppler (1838–1894) studied at the Vienna Academy of Fine Arts. In 1872 he moved to New York to work for *Leslie's Weekly*. With Adolph Schwartzmann he launched the American version of *Puck* in 1877.

Maurice Ketten (1875–1965) studied at the Ecole des Beaux Arts in Paris and emigrated to the United States in 1898. He worked for the *Denver Post* before drawing several successful comic strips for the *New York Evening World*.

Rudolph E. Leppert (1872–1949) studied at the Art Students' League in New York and spent 1900–02 as a cartoonist for the *Anaconda Standard* before joining the *New York Herald*. His cartoons also appeared in the *New York Evening World* and *Harper's*.

Albert Levering (1869–1929) studied art in Munich and contributed cartoons to the *Minneapolis Times*, *Chicago Tribune*, *New York American*, *Puck*, *Harper's Weekly*, and *Life*.

Ferdinand G. Long (1868–1948) worked for thirty years as a cartoonist for the *New York Evening World*, spent two years on the staff of the *London Express*, and was a contributor to *Life*.

Amédée Ernest Lynen (1852–1938) was a staff artist for the Belgian satiric newspaper *Le Diable au Corps* and illustrated the *Guide de la section de l'état indépendant du Congo à l'exposition de Bruxelles-Tervueren* (1897).

C. R. Macauley (1871–1934), a godson of William McKinley, worked as a freelance cartoonist for the *Cleveland World, Cleveland Plain Dealer, Philadelphia Inquirer, New York Herald, New York World, Brooklyn Eagle, Life*, and *Judge*. He received the Pulitzer Prize for Editorial Cartooning in 1930.

Claude Maybell (1872–1955) studied art at the School of Design in San Francisco. He was a longstanding staff cartoonist for the *Brooklyn Eagle* before moving to a position in advertising.

Henry "Hy" Mayer (1868–1954) was the political editor of the *New York Times* from 1904 to 1914, when he became editor of *Puck*. His drawings were published in the *Fliegende Blätter* in Munich, *Le Figaro* and *Le Rire* in Paris, *Punch* and the *Pall Mall Gazette* in London, and by *Judge, Puck, Life, Truth, Leslie's Weekly, Harper's Weekly*, and *Collier's Weekly*.

Homer McKee (1880–1950) studied at the Chicago Art Institute and contributed to the *Chicago Star* and *Dayton Journal*.

Tyler McWhorter (1869–1947) joined the staff of the *Des Moines Leader* in 1896 and later drew for the *St. Paul Prairie Press* and *St. Paul Dispatch*.

Fred Morgan (1865–1932) was the son of London cartoonist Matt Morgan. He emigrated with his family to the United States in 1870 and from 1888–90 he worked for *Once a Week*. Around 1898 he joined the staff of the *Philadelphia Inquirer*.

Wallace Morgan (1875–1948) studied art at the National Academy of Design and worked for the *New York Sun*. In 1898 he joined the staff of the *New York Herald* and from 1929 to 1936 served as president of the Society of American Illustrators.

Tim Murphy (1865–1929) was a comic actor who worked briefly as draughtsman for the US Patent Office.

Thomas Nast (1840–1902) studied at the National Academy of Design and joined the staff of *Harper's Weekly* in 1862. Nast is best known for his attacks on Tammany Hall and his cartoons in support of Lincoln and Grant.

Frederick Burr Opper (1857–1937) began to contribute sketches to *Wild Oats* and *Leslie's Weekly* in 1877 and was a contributor to *Puck* for two decades. In 1900 he worked for the *New York Journal-American*.

Richard F. Outcault (1863–1928), best known for creating the "Yellow Kid" and "Buster Brown" cartoon strips, was educated at McMicken University School of Design in Cincinnati. He also contributed cartoons to the *New York World* and *Chicago Inter-Ocean* and in 1896 joined the staff of the *New York Journal*.

Albert Reid (1873–1955) studied at the Art Students' League in New York and contributed cartoons to the *Kansas City Journal, Kansas City Star, Chicago Record, New York Herald, Judge, McClure's*, and *Saturday Evening Post*.

Charles S. Reinhart (1844–1896), nephew of painter Benjamin Franklin Reinhart, studied art in Paris and Munich and joined the staff of Harper and Brothers in 1870.

Louis Rhead (1857–1926) studied at the National Art Training School in London. In 1883 he worked as art director for D. Appleton & Co. Rhead created nearly a hundred posters for such magazines as *Cassell's*, *Century*, *Harper's*, and *Scribner's*.

F. T. Richards (1864–1921) studied with Thomas Eakins at the Pennsylvania Academy of Fine Arts and worked for three years in the studio of Edmund Birckhead Bensell, one of the founders of the Philadelphia Sketch Club. He also contributed to *Life*, *Harper's Weekly*, *Collier's Weekly*, the *New York Herald*, the *New York Times*, and the *New York Evening Mail*.

W. A. Rogers (1854–1931) joined the staff of the *New York Daily Graphic* in 1873. He worked for *Harper's Weekly* for a quarter century beginning in 1877. He then worked for the *New York Herald* for twenty years, followed by a stint with the *Washington Post*. He also contributed cartoons to *Life* and *Puck*.

Gordon Ross (1873–1946) first worked as a newspaper illustrator in San Francisco then moved to New York and drew for the *New York Times* and *Puck*.

George Sanglier (1879–1962) was a staff illustrator for the *St. Paul Pioneer Press*.

Modest Stein (1871–1958) emigrated to the United States in 1888 and fell in with New York anarchists in the circle of his cousin Alexander Berkman and Emma Goldman. He was an illustrator and cartoonist for the *New York Herald*, the *New York World*, and *Munsey's*.

Frederick Strothmann (1872–1958) attended Carl Hecker Art School (New York) and continued his studies at the Berlin Royal Academy and in Paris. Strothmann was a staff artist for *Harper's Monthly* from 1906 to 1912 and contributed to *Life* and *Collier's*. He illustrated several of Twain's books in the 1903 edition of his works.

James Guilford "Jimmy" Swinnerton (1875–1974) studied at the San Francisco School of Design. He produced a weekly comic strip entitled "The Little Bears" for the San Francisco *Examiner* then relocated to New York in 1896 to work for another Hearst paper, the *Journal*.

C. J. Taylor (1855–1929) studied at the New York Art Students' League and National Academy of Design. He joined the staff of the *New York Daily Graphic* in 1873 and moved to *Puck* in 1886. He later served as an instructor at the Carnegie Institute of Technology in Pittsburgh.

Willis Hale Thorndike (1872–1940) studied at the San Francisco Art School, Art Students' League in New York, and Académie Julian in Paris. From 1890 to 1892 he worked for the *San Francisco Chronicle* and joined the *Baltimore American* staff in 1906. His cartoons also appeared in the *New York Herald*, *Anaconda Standard*, and *New York World-Telegram*.

Tom Thurlby (1876–1928) was a self-taught artist who worked for the *St. Louis Republic*,

Butte Reveille, Minneapolis Star-Tribune, St. Paul Globe, Kansas City Times, Seattle Times, and *Seattle Post-Intelligencer.*

Floyd Wilding Triggs (1872–1919) was an artist and cartoonist born in Winnebago, Illinois. He studied art at the Art Institute in Chicago and worked for the *Minneapolis Tribune, Chicago Daily News, New York Press,* and *Christian Science Monitor.*

Alexander Josef Van Leshout (1868–1930) studied art in Paris and with painter Carroll Beckwith. He worked for the *Philadelphia Press, Washington Times,* New York *Press, Chicago Tribune, Chicago Inter-Ocean,* and *Louisville Courier-Journal.*

Jean Villemot (1880–1958) contributed to *Le Pêle-mêle, Le Frou-frou, Le Sourire, Le Rire,* and *l'Assiette au Beurre.*

William Henry Walker (1871–1938), educated at the Art Students' League in New York, was a regular contributor to *Life, Harper's,* the *New York Evening Post,* and the *New York Herald.*

Leslie Ward ("Spy") (1851–1922) was born in London into a family of painters. He studied at the Royal Academy of Art and joined the staff of *Vanity Fair* in 1873, for which he produced over a thousand caricatures by 1911.

Rudolf Wetterau (1892–1953) was an artist and cartoonist for the *Nashville American.*

Truman W. ("True") Williams (1839–1897) was the primary illustrator of *The Innocents Abroad* (1869) and *Roughing It* (1872) and sole illustrator of *The Adventures of Tom Sawyer* (1876) and *Sketches, New and Old* (1875).

David Wilson (1873–1935) studied at the Government School of Art in Belfast and placed his first drawing in the *London Chronicle* in 1895. He published widely in illustrated weeklies such as *Punch, Graphic, Fun, London Opinion, Sketch,* and *Life.*

Frank Wing (1873–1956) was a staff cartoonist for the *Minneapolis Journal.* He also contributed to the *Minneapolis Tribune, St. Paul Pioneer Press,* and *Chicago Tribune.* Late in life he mentored "Peanuts" cartoonist Charles Schulz.

Art Young (1866–1943) studied at the Chicago Academy of Design, Académie Julian in Paris, and the Art Students' League in New York. He contributed to the *Chicago Evening Mail, Chicago Tribune, Chicago Inter-Ocean, New York Evening Herald, New York American, Life,* and *Puck.*

Notes

Introduction

1. Brooks [Hawkins], "Something About Models," *Brooklyn Eagle*, 20 August 1905, 13.
2. Bush, Courtney, and Messent, eds., *The Letters of Mark Twain and Joseph Hopkins Twichell* (Athens: Univ. of Georgia Press, 2017), 197.
3. Atherton, "Post-Mortem Appreciation," *Appleton's Booklovers* 1 (March 1903), 239.
4. Salamo and Smith, eds., *Mark Twain's Letters* (Berkeley: Univ. of California Press, 1997), vol. 5, 461–62.
5. Mark Twain to David Croly, 13 March 1873 (Mark Twain Papers, UCLC 13509).
6. Scharnhorst and Myrick, "A Note on Mark Twain and Chinese Missions," *American Literary Realism* 54 (Spring 2022), 275–76.
7. Scharnhorst and Myrick, "A Note on Mark Twain and Chinese Missions," 275–76.
8. Mark Twain to Bernhard Tauchnitz, 1 March 1883 (Mark Twain Papers, UCCL 02352).
9. G. E. Stechert & Co. to Mark Twain, 12 July 1905 (Mark Twain Papers, UCLC 34538).
10. "Famous Caricaturist, Albert Scott Cox, Will Test His Art on Boston's Noted Men for Post," *Boston Post*, 25 December 1906, 10.
11. *Sioux City (Iowa) Journal*, 18 June 1950, 10.
12. Paine, *Mark Twain: A Biography* (New York: Harper & Bros., 1912), facing 1130.
13. Scharnhorst, ed., *Mark Twain: The Complete Interviews* (Tuscaloosa: Univ. of Alabama Press, 2006), 526, 528.
14. Budd, "Mark Twain's Visual Humor," in *A Companion to Mark Twain*, ed. Messent and Budd (Malden, Mass.: Blackwell, 2005), 483n10.

1 Mark Twain "on the War Path," 1869

1. Fischer and Frank, eds., *Mark Twain's Letters* (Berkeley: Univ. of California Press, 1992), vol. 3, 139.
2. Twain, *The Innocents Abroad* (Hartford: American Publishing Co., 1869), 124.
3. Paine, ed., *Mark Twain's Letters* (New York: Harper & Bros., 1917), 272.

2 Mark Twain and Moving Day, 1880

1. Scharnhorst, ed., *Mark Twain: The Complete Interviews*, 18.
2. "Cartoons and Comments," *Puck*, 28 April 1880, 124; "Strength with a Difference," *Puck*, 4 February 1880, 777.
3. "Mr. H. Bug as a Humanitarian," *Puck*, 29 October 1879, 537.

3 Mark Twain and the Campaign for International Copyright, 1882–1907

1. "Prince and Pauper," *Washington Critic*, 20 December 1881, 1; *Springfield Republican*, 17 December 1881, 4.
2. Budd, *Our Mark Twain* (Philadelphia: Univ. of Pennsylvania Press, 1983), 76.
3. "The Oath of the House Combine," *St. Louis Post-Dispatch*, 9 September 1902, 1.
4. Scharnhorst, ed., *Mark Twain: The Complete Interviews*, 572; Twain, "Concerning Copyright," *North American Review* 180 (January 1905), 1–8.
5. Griffin et al., eds., *Autobiography of Mark Twain* (Berkeley: Univ. of California Press, 2013), vol. 2, 338.
6. Mark Twain to Champ Clark, 5 June 1909 (Mark Twain Papers, UCCL 08415).

4 Mark Twain and the Concord School of Philosophy, 1883

1. Smith et al., eds., *Autobiography of Mark Twain* (Berkeley: Univ. of California Press, 2010), vol. 1, 261.

5 Mark Twain the Satirist, 1891

1. Beard, *Hardly a Man Is Now Alive* (New York: Doubleday, Doran, 1939), 336–37; "Mark Twain and His Illustrator," *Success* 3 (June 1900), 205.
2. Paine, *Mark Twain: A Biography*, 888.
3. Camfield, *The Oxford Companion to Mark Twain* (New York: Oxford Univ. Press, 2003), 134.
4. Mark Twain to Dan Beard, 28 August 1889 (Mark Twain Papers, UCCL 03933).
5. Inge, "Beard, Daniel Carter," in *The Routledge Encyclopedia of Mark Twain*, ed. LeMaster and Wilson (New York: Routledge, 2011), 64.
6. Mark Twain to Dan Beard, 11 November 1889 (Mark Twain Papers, UCCL 03965).
7. Mark Twain to L. E. Parkhurst, 20 December 1889 (Mark Twain Papers, UCCL 03991).
8. Fatout, ed., *Mark Twain Speaking* (Iowa City: Univ. of Iowa Press, 1976), 473–74.
9. Twain, *A Connecticut Yankee in King Arthur's Court* (New York: Webster, 1889), 511.
10. Twain, *A Connecticut Yankee*, 573.
11. Twain, "Travelling with a Reformer," *Cosmopolitan* 16 (December 1893), 207, 217.

6 Mark Twain in Australia, 1895

1. *Adelaide South Australian Advertiser*, 14 September 1887, 5.
2. *Sydney Telegraph*, 17 September 1895, 5.
3. *Sydney Australian Star*, 17 September 1895, 4.
4. "Mark Twain," *Sydney Telegraph*, 19 September 1895, 5.
5. "Our Telephone," *Sydney Times*, 22 September 1895, 5.

8 Mark Twain and Language Reform, 1897–1907

1. Twain, *A Tramp Abroad* (Hartford: American Publishing Co., 1880), 604–6, 608, 618.
2. Translated in *New York Journal and Advertiser*, 21 November 1897, 33.
3. Twain, *The Innocents Abroad*, 645.
4. Paine, ed., *Mark Twain's Letters* (New York: Harper & Bros., 1917), 357–59.

5. Twain, *Sketches New and Old* (Hartford: American Publishing Co., 1875), 101, 107.

6. Twain, *The $30,000 Bequest and Other Stories* (New York: Harper & Bros., 1906), 171–72.

7. Twain, *What Is Man? and Other Essays* (New York: Harper & Bros., 1917), 256.

8. "Adieu, 'Chauffeur'!" *Harper's Weekly*, 13 January 1906, 58.

9. "The Carnegie Spelling Reform," *Harper's Weekly*, 7 April 1906, 488.

10. "Carnegie, Edison, and Twain," *New York Sun*, 10 December 1907, 4.

11. *New York World*, 15 December 1907, metro section, 1.

9 Mark Twain the Internationalist, 1897–1909

1. Twain, *The Innocents Abroad*, 348.

2. Twain, "Diogenes and His Lantern," *Harper's Weekly*, 12 August 1905, 1166.

3. Fatout, ed., *Mark Twain Speaking*, 323.

4. Fatout, ed., *Mark Twain Speaking*, 293.

5. Paine, ed., *Mark Twain's Letters*, 514.

6. Paine, *Mark Twain: A Biography*, 893.

7. Bridge, *Personal Recollections of Nathaniel Hawthorne* (New York: Harper & Bros., 1893), 112.

8. "A Night in Panama," *Washington Post*, 28 January 1906, 6.

9. Twain, *A Tramp Abroad* (Hartford: American Publishing Co., 1880), 503.

10 Mark Twain the Anti-Imperialist, 1901–08

1. Twain, *Following the Equator* (Hartford: American Publishing Co., 1897), 623.

2. Scharnhorst, ed., *Mark Twain: The Complete Interviews*, 353.

3. *Mark Twain: The Complete Interviews*, 358.

4. Kinzer, *The True Flag: Theodore Roosevelt, Mark Twain, and the Birth of American Empire* (New York: Holt, 2017), 215.

5. Smith et al., eds., *Autobiography of Mark Twain*, vol. 1, 404.

6. Twain, *Collected Tales, Sketches, Speeches, & Essays, 1891–1910* (New York: Library of America, 1992), 473.

7. "Twain Introduces Churchill," *New York Sun*, 13 December 1900, 3.

8. Fatout, ed., *Mark Twain Speaking*, 367.

9. "Twain Introduces Churchill," 3.

10. "Winston Churchill's Lecture," *Brooklyn Eagle*, 13 December 1900, 4.

11. New York *Evening Post*, 13 December 1900, 8.

12. Budd, *Mark Twain: Social Philosopher* (Bloomington: Indiana Univ. Press, 1962), 177.

13. "Mark Twain and His Critics," *Minneapolis Tribune*, 10 March 1901, 6.

14. "Demand That Twain Retract," *New York Tribune*, 22 March 1901, 6.

15. "Mark Twain's 'Apology,'" *New York Tribune*, 30 March 1901, 5.

16. "'Low Birth and Poor Breeding' of Mr. S. L. Clemens," *Boston Globe*, 23 April 1901, 2.

17. "Twain's Retort to Dr. Spaulding," *New York Sun*, 29 April 1901, 1.

18. Harmon and Scharnhorst, "Mark Twain's Interviews: Supplement One," *American Literary Realism* 39 (Spring 2007), 267.

19. *Life*, 14 February 1901, 124.

20. *Book Buyer*, ns 13 (April 1896), 143; *McClure's*, 7 (June 1896), 78; *Idler* 9 (July 1896), 900; London *Review of Reviews*, 16 (August 1897), 122.

21. Quoted in Philip S. Foner, *Mark Twain: Social Critic* (New York: International, 1958), 316.

22. Paine, *Mark Twain: A Biography*, 1283.

23. Gertrude Natkin to Mark Twain, 16 April 1906 (Mark Twain Papers, UCLC 35406).

24. "'Russian Liberty Has Had Its Last Chance,' Says Mark Twain," *Boston Globe*, 30 August 1905, 4.

25. *Mark Twain: The Complete Interviews*, 499, 529.

26. Griffin et al., eds., *Autobiography of Mark Twain*, vol. 2, 134, 307.

27. Kaplan, *Mr. Clemens and Mark Twain* (New York: Simon & Schuster, 1966), 366.

28. Twain, *King Leopold's Soliloquy* (Boston: Warren, 1905), 7, 29, 39, 40.

29. *An Answer to Mark Twain* (Brussels: Bulens, 1907), 5–6.

30. "Mark Twain," *London Chronicle*, 2 July 1907, 7; *Mark Twain: The Complete Interviews*, 633–34.

11 Mark Twain's Return to the United States in 1900

1. "Mark Twain Coming to Run for President," *New York World*, 5 May 1900, 1.

2. *New York Press*; rpt. "Twain for President," *Salt Lake Herald*, 17 May 1900, 4.

3. *Mark Twain Speaking*, 350.

4. *Mark Twain Speaking*, 351.

12 Mark Twain vs. the Cabman, 1900

1. Twain, *The Man That Corrupted Hadleyburg and Other Stories and Essays* (New York: Harper & Bros., 1900), 349.

2. Paine, *Mark Twain: A Biography*, 1125.

3. "Mark Twain in Vienna," *Louisville Courier-Journal*, 12 March 1899, 22.

4. Lawton, *A Lifetime with Mark Twain: The Memories of Katy Leary* (New York: Harcourt, Brace, 1925), 198.

5. Lawton, *A Lifetime with Mark Twain*, 198.

6. "Mark Twain Defies Cabman," *New York Evening World*, 22 November 1900, 1.

7. *Mark Twain: The Complete Interviews*, 379.

8. *Mark Twain: The Complete Interviews*, 380–81.

9. "Lotos Club's Welcome to the Governor," *New York Times*, 24 March 1901, 2.

10. "A Cabman's Estimate of Twain," *New York Tribune*, 2 May 1901, 5.

11. Lawton, *A Lifetime with Mark Twain*, 199–200.

13 Mark Twain's Campaign against Tammany Hall, 1901

1. *Mark Twain: The Complete Interviews*, 401.

2. "Mark Twain's Return to Humor," *Chicago Tribune*, 26 March 1901, 6.

3. "Low Will Construe Laws in a Broad, Liberal Way," *Brooklyn Eagle*, 29 October 1901, 1.

4. Hill, *Mark Twain: God's Fool* (New York: Harper & Row, 1973), 39.

5. "The 'Acorns' Hold an Election Jubilee," *New York Times*, 7 November 1901, 3.

6. Budd, *Mark Twain: Social Philosopher*, 199.

14 Mark Twain on Christian Science and Mary Baker Eddy, 1902-07

1. Olivia Langdon Clemens to Alice Hooker Day, 4 February 1894 (Mark Twain Papers, UCCL 10520).
2. Mark Twain to Edward Everett Hale, 1 November 1899 (Mark Twain Papers, UCCL 05698).
3. Mark Twain to Edward Day, 21 March 1903 (Mark Twain Papers, UCCL 06606).
4. Mark Twain to John Greenall, 6 April 1906 (Mark Twain Papers, UCCL 08891).
5. "Mrs. Eddy's Writings," *Harper's Weekly*, 24 January 1903, 147.
6. *Brooklyn Eagle*, 13 May 1907, 26.
7. "Mark Twain Fuss at Actors' Fair," *New York Times*, 1 May 1907, 2.
8. "Nice Little Row over Mark Twain," *Hartford Courant*, 3 May 1907, 9.
9. "New York Letter," *Cleveland Plain Dealer*, 11 May 1907, 4.
10. *New York Tribune*, 7 May 1907, 4.
11. Barrymore, *Memories* (New York: Harper & Bros., 1955), 154-55.
12. "Mrs. Rosenfeld Out," *New York Tribune*, 11 May 1907, 10.
13. Twain, *Christian Science* (New York: Harper & Bros., 1907), 285.

15 Mark Twain and Censorship, 1906-07

1. "Huck Finn Tabooed by Denver," *Washington Times*, 7 September 1902, 24.
2. "Mark Twain Scores Men Who Don't Like 'Huck,'" *Denver Post*, 18 August 1902, 1.
3. Mark Twain to Asa Dickinson, 21 November 1905 (Mark Twain Papers, UCCL 07215).
4. Mark Twain to Harriet Whitmore, 7 February 1907 (Mark Twain Papers, UCCL 07645).
5. Irvin Alexander to Mark Twain, 30 March 1906 (Mark Twain Papers, UCLC 35361).
6. "Raps Library Commission," *Detroit Free Press*, 24 April 1907, 5.
7. Carlton, San Francisco *Call*, 12 May 1907, 52.

16 Mark Twain Among the Plutocrats, 1906-08

1. York, Penn., *Daily*, 29 April 1908, 7.
2. Benjamin Griffin and Harriet Elinor Smith, eds. *Autobiography of Mark Twain* (Berkeley: Univ. of California Press, 2015), vol. 3, 183, 189.
3. "Sharp Price Recovery," *New York Tribune*, 21 August 1907, 2.

17 The Man in the White Flannel Suit and Dress Reform, 1907

1. Wiggin, *My Garden of Memory* (Boston: Houghton Mifflin, 1923), 307.
2. Twain, "Chapters from My Autobiography," *North American Review*, 5 April 1907, 676.
3. Griffin et al., *Autobiography of Mark Twain*, vol. 2, 249-50.
4. Flagg, *Roses and Buckshot* (New York: Putnam's, 1946), 168-70.
5. "Earl Grey Banqueted in New York," *Sheffield Telegraph*, 2 April 1906, 6.
6. *Mark Twain: The Complete Interviews*, 556, 562-63.
7. Griffin et al., *Autobiography of Mark Twain*, vol. 3, 253.
8. Howells, *My Mark Twain* (New York: Harper & Bros., 1910), 96.
9. Mark Twain to Jean Clemens, 7 December 1906 (Mark Twain Papers, UCLC 07582).

10. "The Contrast," *Minneapolis Star Tribune*, 7 March 1907, 4.
11. George Smalley to Mark Twain, 28 June 1907 (Mark Twain Papers, UCLC 36822).
12. Ward, *Forty Years of "Spy"* (London: Chatto & Windus, 1915), 129.

18 Obituary Cartoons, 1910

1. Inge, "Comics," in *Mark Twain Encyclopedia*, 168.
2. Budd, *Our Mark Twain*, 12.

Afterword

1. Bush, *Mark Twain and the Spiritual Crisis of His Age* (Tuscaloosa: Univ. of Alabama Press, 2007), 274–75.

Bibliography

Primary Works

Bush, Harold K., Steve Courtney, Peter Messent, eds. *The Letters of Mark Twain and Joseph Hopkins Twichell*. Athens: Univ. of Georgia Press, 2017.
Fatout, Paul, ed. *Mark Twain Speaking*. Iowa City: Univ. of Iowa Press, 1976.
Fischer, Victor, and Michael Frank, eds. *Mark Twain's Letters*. Vol. 3. Berkeley: Univ. of California Press, 1992.
Griffin, Benjamin, et al., eds. *Autobiography of Mark Twain*. Vol. 2. Berkeley: Univ. of California Press, 2013.
Griffin, Benjamin, et al., eds. *Autobiography of Mark Twain*. Vol. 3. Berkeley: Univ. of California Press, 2015.
Paine, A. B., ed. *Mark Twain's Letters*. New York: Harper & Bros, 1917.
Salamo, Lin, and Harriet Elinor Smith, eds. *Mark Twain's Letters*. Vol. 5. Berkeley: Univ. of California Press, 1997.
Scharnhorst, Gary, ed. *Mark Twain: The Complete Interviews*. Tuscaloosa: Univ. of Alabama Press, 2006.
Smith, Harriet Elinor, et al., eds., *Autobiography of Mark Twain*. Vol. 1. Berkeley: Univ. of California Press, 2010.
Twain, Mark. *The Innocents Abroad*. Hartford: American Publishing Co., 1869.
_____. *Sketches New and Old*. Hartford: American Publishing Co., 1875.
_____. *A Tramp Abroad*. Hartford: American Publishing Co., 1880.
_____. *A Connecticut Yankee in King Arthur's Court*. New York: Webster, 1889.
_____. *Following the Equator*. Hartford: American Publishing Co., 1897.
_____. *The Man That Corrupted Hadleyburg and Other Stories and Essays*. New York: Harper & Bros., 1900.
_____. "Concerning Copyright." *North American Review*. January 1905.
_____. *King Leopold's Soliloquy*. Boston: Warren, 1905.
_____. *Christian Science*. New York: Harper & Bros., 1907.
_____. *The $30,000 Bequest and Other Stories*. New York: Harper & Bros., 1917.
_____. *Collected Tales, Sketches, Speeches, & Essays*. Edited by Louis J. Budd. New York: Library of America, 1992.

Major Secondary Sources

An Answer to Mark Twain. Brussels: Bulens, 1907.
Barrymore, Ethel. *Memories*. New York: Harper & Bros., 1955.
Beard, Dan. *Hardly a Man Is Now Alive*. New York: Doubleday, Doran, 1939.
Budd, Louis J. *Mark Twain: Social Philosopher*. Bloomington: Indiana Univ. Press, 1962.
_____. *Our Mark Twain*. Philadelphia: Univ. of Pennsylvania Press, 1983.

Bush, Harold K. *Mark Twain and the Spiritual Crisis of His Age*. Tuscaloosa: Univ. of Alabama Press, 2007.

Camfield, Greg. *The Oxford Companion to Mark Twain*. New York: Oxford Univ. Press, 2003.

Foner, Philip S., *Mark Twain: Social Critic*. New York: International, 1958.

Hill, Hamlin. *Mark Twain: God's Fool*. New York: Harper & Row, 1973.

Howells, W. D. *My Mark Twain*. New York: Harper & Bros., 1910.

Kaplan, Justin. *Mr. Clemens and Mark Twain*. New York: Simon & Schuster, 1966.

Kinzer, Stephen. *The True Flag: Theodore Roosevelt, Mark Twain, and the Birth of American Empire*. New York: Holt, 2017.

Lawton, Mary. *A Lifetime with Mark Twain: The Memories of Katy Leary*. New York: Harcourt, Brace, 1925.

LeMaster, J. R., and James D. Wilson, eds. *The Routledge Encyclopedia of Mark Twain*. New York: Routledge, 2011.

Messent, Peter, and Louis J. Budd, ed. *A Companion to Mark Twain*. Malden, Mass.: Blackwell, 2005.

Paine, A. B. *Mark Twain: A Biography*. New York: Harper & Bros., 1912.

Ward, Leslie. *Forty Years of "Spy."* London: Chatto & Windus, 1915.

Wiggin, Kate Douglas. *My Garden of Memory*. Boston: Houghton Mifflin, 1923.

Manuscripts

Mark Twain Papers, Bancroft Library, University of California, Berkeley.

Index

Académie Julian, 102, 104, 105
Actors' Fund Fair, 78–80
Alcott, Bronson, 19
Alcott, Louisa May, 19
Aldrich, Thomas B., 64
Alexander II, Czar, 56
Alexander VI, Czar, 58
Alexander, Irvin, 81, 82, 101
Ament, William Scott, 45, 52, 53
American Anti-Imperialist League, 45
American Copyright League, 14
American Publishing Co., 7, 107–9
Anaconda Standard, 73, 102, 104
Anderson, Jesse S. "Vet," 50, 51, 101
Answer to Mark Twain, An, 59, 60
Anthony, Susan B., 19, 21
anti-imperialism, Mark Twain's, 2, 4, 43–62
Appleton's Booklovers, 3, 107
Assiette au Beurre, l', 59, 60
Atherton, Gertrude, 2, 107
Australia, 25–26, 39
Australian Star, 26

Bacon, Francis, 1
Baker, Edith, 78, 79
Bangs, John Kendrick, 27, 28
Barnett, H. Walter, 55
Barr, Amelia E. H., 27, 28
Barrymore, Ethel, 80
Bartholomew, Charles Lewis "Bart," 50, 73, 74, 101
Barton, Edmund, 26
Beard, Dan, 22–24, 101
Beck, William, 66–68, 70
Beckwith, Carroll, 105
Beecher, Henry Ward, 10, 11
Beelzebub, 40
Belford Brothers, 12
Bellerophon, 2, 3

Bengough, William, 30, 31, 101
Bensell, Edmund Birckhead, 104
Bentzon, Th., 32, 33
Bergh, Henry, 10, 11
Berkman, Alexander, 104
Berryman, Clifford K., 41, 92, 101
Bixby, Horace, 77
Blaine, James G., 10
Blanc, Marie-Thérèse. *See* Bentzon, Th.
Bliss, Elisha, Jr., 4
Blix, Ragnvald, 5
Boer War, 44–45
Book Buyer, 55
Bookman (New York), 45, 47
Boston Herald, 39, 101, 110
Bowman, Rowland C., 49, 71, 101
Boxer Rebellion, 1, 45, 53
Briggs, Clare, 96. 97, 101
British Parliament, 16, 44
Brooklyn Clerical Union, 51–52
Brooklyn Eagle, 72, 103, 107, 109
Browning, Robert, 14, 15, 58
Budd, Louis J., 6, 12, 45, 75, 96, 107–9, 111–14
Bulkeley, Morgan, 4
Burnett, Frances Hodgson, 27, 28
Burns, Ken, 6
Bush, Harold K., 99, 107, 112, 113, 114
Butler, Benjamin, 10, 11, 19, 21
Byrne, Michael, 67

Cable, George Washington, 14, 15
Canadian Department of Agriculture and Arts, 12–14
Cannon, Joseph, 41
Carlton, Will, 14
Carnegie, Andrew, 36–37, 62, 84, 85, 86, 87
Carroll, Lewis, 14, 15
Cartoonists' Beefsteak Supper, 84
Cedar Rapids Gazette, 96, 102

censorship, Mark Twain on, 81–83
Century Theatre Club, 78–79
Cesare, Oscar, 37, 101
Chapin, Archibald B., 92, 93, 101
Chatto, Andrew, 40
Chatto & Windus, 12, 112, 114
Chicago Art Institute, 103, 105
Chicago Daily News, 83, 101, 105
Chicago Evening Mail, 105
Chicago Inter-Ocean, 16, 101, 103, 105
Chicago Tribune, 24, 71, 96, 97, 101, 102, 105, 110
China, 1, 45, 49–50
Christian Science, 4, 61, 76–80
Churchill, Winston Spencer, 44–45
Clark, Champ, 18, 108
Clemens, Clara, 25, 96
Clemens, Jean, 63, 90, 112
Clemens, Olivia Langdon (Livy), 7, 25, 32, 33, 76, 111
Clemens, Olivia Susan (Susy), 76
Clemens, Samuel L. *See* Twain, Mark
Cleveland, Grover, 39
Cleveland Plain Dealer, 80, 103, 111
Collins, Wilkie, 2, 14, 15
Columbia (personification), 97
Comstock, Anthony, 9, 10
Concord School of Philosophy, 19–21
Congo Free State, 58–62
Congo Reform Association, 58, 59
Conkling, Roscoe, 10, 11
copyright reform, 4, 9, 12–18, 88
Cory, John Campbell, 84, 101
Cox, Albert Scott, 5, 101
Critic (Washington, DC), 12
Croly, David, 4
Cutter, Bloodgood, 56

David, Beverly R., 6
Davis, Richard Harding, 28, 29
Day, Alice Hooker, 76
Denver Post, 81, 102
Denver Public Library, 81
Depew, Chauncey, 64, 69
Des Moines Leader, 3, 103
Detroit, Mich., 83
Detroit Free Press, 62, 101
Dewey, George, 44, 55, 63
Dickinson, Anna E., 10, 11

Diogenes of Sinope, 38
dress reform, Mark Twain on, 88–95
Duncan, Dayton, 6
Dunne, Finley Peter, 62
Dwiggins, Clare "Dwig," 58, 59, 65, 66, 67, 102

Eakins, Thomas, 104
Ebert, Charles Henry, 77, 102
Eddy, Mary Baker, 61, 62, 76–80
Edison, Thomas, 10
Edward, King, 58, 59
Emerson, Ralph Waldo, 19
Evansville Courier, 82
Evarts, William M., 19, 20

Figaro (London), 4
Flagg, James Montgomery, 88
Fliegende Blätter, 4, 103
Floh, Der, 5, 38, 102
Florence, Italy, 33
Ford, Lorenzo W., 52, 53, 102
free silver movement, 27, 63, 64
free trade, 25–26
Freeman, Mary E. Wilkins, 27, 28
French Congo League, 59
Frohman, Daniel, 77, 78
Frueh, Al, 92, 94, 102
Fun, 4

Gilbert, W. S., 12, 14
Goldman, Emma, 104
Gorky, Maxim, 1
Gould, Francis Carruthers, 23, 58, 102
Gould, Jay, 9, 10
Graetz, Friedrich, 38, 102
Grant, Ulysses S., 9, 10, 11, 103
Greeley, Horace, 11
Grey, Earl, 88
Gridiron Club, 41
Guayana Esequiba, 39

Hanna, Mark, 54, 56
Hardy, Thomas, 14, 15
Harper & Brothers, 33, 76, 104
Harper's Bazar, 29
Harper's Monthly, 27, 101, 104
Harper's Weekly, 2, 4, 5, 12, 13, 18, 34, 35, 38, 46, 61, 73, 76, 78, 102–4
Harriman, E. H., 86, 87

Harrison, Benjamin, 54
Harte, Bret, 14, 15
Harvey, George, 63
Harvey, William "Coin," 27, 28
Hawkins, Willis Brooks, 1, 2
Hawthorne, Julian, 28, 29
Hawthorne, Nathaniel, 40
Hawthorne, Sophia, 29
Hill, David B., 27, 28
Hill, James J., 62
Holmes, Oliver Wendell, 14, 15, 19, 21
Hopkins, Livingston "Hop," 25, 26, 102
Howells, W. D., 8, 14, 15, 28, 29, 40, 64, 69, 88, 90
Hruska, James, J., 96, 102

Idler (London), 55
India, 1, 33
Indianapolis Star, 35
Inge, M. Thomas, 22, 96
international copyright, 4, 9, 12–17, 88
Italy, 33

Joan of Arc, 27, 45, 76
Joy, Richard, 83

Kansas City Journal, 52, 103
Kansas City Star, 101, 103
Kansas City Times, 24, 105
Kaplan, Justin, 58
Kearney, Denis, 10
Kelley, John, 10, 11
Kendrick, Charles, 21, 102
Keppler, Joseph, 14, 15, 102
Ketten, Maurice, 79, 102
Kikeriki, 5, 102
Kipling, Rudyard, 39

language reform, Mark Twain on, 30–37
Leary, Katy, 66, 70
Leopold II, King of Belgium, 38, 58–62
Leppert, Rudolph E., 73, 102
Levering, Albert, 33, 34, 77, 78, 102
Lewis, Fred E., 5
Life, 16–17, 19–21, 27, 28, 42, 45, 48, 55, 66, 76, 77, 102, 103, 104
Lincoln, Abraham, 103
London, England, 12, 39, 55, 63, 66, 85, 94
London Authors' Club, 39

London Chronicle, 61
London *Review of Reviews*, 55
London Royal Literary Fund, 63
Long, Ferdinand G., 63, 68, 102
Lotos Club, 64, 69
Low, Seth, 71, 72, 75
Lowell, James Russell, 14, 15
Lynen, Amédée Ernest, 60, 103
Lyon, Isabel, 81

Macauley, C. R., 56, 57, 64, 86, 87, 103
Mark Twain House and Museum, Hartford, 5
Mark Twain Papers, Berkeley, 5
Matthews, Brander, 27, 28
May, Phil, 102
Maybell, Claude, 72, 103
Mayer, Henry "Hy," 36, 103
McClure's, 55, 62, 103
McKee, Homer, 33, 35, 103
McKinley, William, 27, 28, 38, 54, 55, 103
McWhorter, Tyler, 2, 3, 23, 36, 103
Meltzer, Milton, 6
Metropolitan Museum, New York, 85, 86
Metropolitan Opera House, New York, 78
Mille, Pierre, 59, 60
Minneapolis Journal, 50, 74, 101
Minneapolis Tribune, 45, 49, 71, 74, 101
missionaries, 45, 49–52
Missouri House of Delegates, 15–16
Monroe Doctrine, 39
Morel, E. D., 59, 60
Morgan, Frederick Summerville, 84, 85, 103
Morgan, J. Pierpont, 62, 85, 86, 87
Morgan, Matt, 103
Morgan, Wallace, 89, 103
Murphy, Tim, 23, 45, 47, 103
Museum of the City of New York, 37

Nankivell, Frank, 5
Nashville American, 96, 97, 105
Nast, Thomas, 2, 12, 13–14, 73, 103
Natkin, Gertrude, 56
Neues Wiener Tageblatt, 30
New York American, 102
New York Art Students' League, 101–5
New York Clerical Union, 51, 52
New York Daily Graphic, 4, 104
New York Evening Journal, 30, 32, 102
New York Evening Post, 45, 101, 103, 105

New York Evening World, 63, 66, 68, 79, 102
New York Herald, 51, 68, 88–89, 93, 101–5
New York Journal and Advertiser, 30, 31
New York Press, 63, 85, 86, 105
New York Public Library, 36
New York Sun, 44, 45, 103
New York Times, 5, 80, 101, 103, 104
New York Tribune, 27, 50, 94
New York World, 9, 56, 69, 84, 87, 90, 101–4
New Zealand, 25
Nicholas II, Czar, 38, 56–57
North American Review, 16, 45, 50, 54, 56, 88
Nye, Edgar Wilson "Bill," 27

obituary cartoons, 96–97
Odell, Benjamin B., Jr., 63
Opper, Frederick Burr, 9–10, 27, 28, 54, 103
Order of Acorns, 72, 75
Outcault, Richard F., 68, 103
Oxford University, 85, 94

Paine, Albert Bigelow, 5, 56
Paine, Thomas, 23
Parkes, Sir Henry, 25–26
Pegasus, 2, 36
Peking Missionary Association, 50
Perth Western Mail, 58
Phelps, Elizabeth Stuart, 28, 29
Philadelphia Inquirer, 64, 65, 67, 84, 85, 102, 103
Philadelphia Sketch Club, 104
Philippine-American War, 1, 43, 44–45, 49, 52–55
Pittsburgh, Pa., 92, 93
Plato, 19
Players' Club, 78
Pond, James B., 44
Puck, 5, 9, 10, 11, 15, 28, 102–5
Punch, 4, 103, 105

Quaker City excursion, 32, 56
Quimby, Phineas P., 76
Quintard, Edward, 96

Reed, Thomas B., 64
Reid, Albert, 51, 52, 103
Reid, Whitelaw, 27
Reinhart, Benjamin Franklin, 104
Reinhart, Charles S., 2, 104

Revue des deux mondes, 32
Rhead, Louis, 48, 104
Richards, F. T., 5, 27, 28, 104
Rockefeller, John D., 62
Rockefeller, John D., Jr., 86, 87
Rogers, Henry Huddleston, 64, 84–85, 86, 87
Rogers, W. A., 45, 46, 64, 104
Roosevelt, Theodore, 38, 41, 54, 64, 86
Root, Elihu, 41
Rosenfeld, Genie Holtzmeyer, 78, 79, 80
Ross, Gordon, 23, 62, 80, 104
Russo-Japanese War, 56

San Francisco Examiner, 54, 104
San Francisco Morning Call, 1
San Francisco School of Design, 104
Sanglier, George, 91, 104
Sarony, Napoleon, 5
Schulz, Charles, 105
Schwartzmann, Adolph, 102
Shakespeare, William, 1, 51
Shakespeare-Bacon debate, 1
Shepard, Edward M., 71, 72, 73
Simplicissimus, 5
simplified spelling, 33, 36, 37
Smalley, George, 94
Smith, Francis Hopkinson, 27, 28
Society for the Suppression of Noise, 1, 9
South Africa, 1, 44–45
Spanish-American War, 44
Spaulding, Wayland, 51
Springfield Republican, 12
Standard Oil Company, 84
Stein, Modest, 90, 104
Stevenson, Robert Louis, 14, 15
St. Louis Post-Dispatch, 92, 94, 102, 103
Stockton, Frank, 14, 15
Stockton Record, 40
Stowe, Harriet Beecher, 16
St. Paul Globe, 53, 75, 105
St. Paul Pioneer Press, 91, 104, 105
Strothmann, Frederick, 33, 34, 104
Success, 59
Such, B. J., 12
Sullivan, Arthur, 13, 14
Sullivan, John L., 19–20
Swinnerton, James "Jimmy," 30, 32, 104
Sydney Australian Star, 26
Sydney Telegraph, 25

Sydney Times, 26
Syracuse Evening Herald, 53, 102

Taft, William Howard, 41
Talmage, De Witt, 10, 11
Tammany Hall, 2, 9–10, 71–75, 103
Tauchnitz, Bernhard, 4
Taylor, C. J., 92, 93, 104
Tennyson, Alfred Lord, 14, 15
Thoreau, Henry David, 19
Thorndike, Willis Hale, 39, 104
Thurlby, Tom, 73, 75, 104–5
Tilden, Samuel, 10, 11
Topeka Herald, 93
transcendentalism, 19
Treaty of Paris, 44
Treaty of Portsmouth, 56
Triggs, Floyd Wilding, 85, 86, 105
trusts, 54
Twain, Mark, writings by:
—*Adventures of Huckleberry Finn*, 81
—*Adventures of Tom Sawyer, The*, 8, 12, 15, 16, 81, 90
—"Awful German Language, The," 30, 33;
—"Carnegie's Spelling Reform," 36
—*Christian Science*, 61, 79, 80
—"Concerning Copyright," 16
—*Connecticut Yankee in King Arthur's Court, A*, 22–23, 40, 99
—"Czar's Soliloquy, The," 56–57, 58, 99
—*Double-Barreled Detective Story, A*, 83
—*Editorial Wild Oats*, 33
—*Extracts from Adam's Diary*, 33
—*Following the Equator*, 43, 45, 109
—*Gilded Age, The*, 4
—"Horrors of the German Language, The," 30
—*Innocents Abroad, The*, 7–8, 32, 38, 45, 96, 105
—*Is Shakespeare Dead?* 1
—"Italian Without a Master," 33
—"Jim Smiley and His Jumping Frog," 32
—"'Jumping Frog' in English, then in French, then Clawed Back, The," 32–33, 34
—"King Leopold's Soliloquy," 58–62, 99
—*Personal Recollections of Joan of Arc*, 27, 45
—*Prince and the Pauper, The*, 12, 13
—*Pudd'nhead Wilson*, 86
—"Schrecken der deutchen Sprache, Die," 30

—*Sketches New and Old*, 32
—"To My Missionary Critics," 50
—"To the Person Sitting in Darkness," 45, 49, 52, 54, 55, 99
—*Tramp Abroad, A*, 12, 30, 42
—"Travelling with a Reformer," 23
—"Whittier Birthday Speech," 1, 19
Twichell, Joseph Hopkins, 1

Ulk, 4
Uncle Tom's Cabin, 16

Vanderbilt, W. H., 10
Vanity Fair, 94–95, 105
Van Leshout, Alexander Josef, 16, 105
van Steinle, Eduard, 102
Venezuela and British Guiana, border dispute, 39
Verne, Jules, 14, 15
Vienna, Austria, 4, 66
Viennese Press Club, 30
Villemot, Jean, 59, 60, 105
vivisection, 1

Walker, William Henry, 55, 105
Ward, Artemus, 27
Ward, Geoffrey C., 6
Ward, Leslie, 94, 95, 105
Warner, Charles Dudley, 14, 15
Washington, Booker T., 64
Washington Post, 41, 101, 104
Washington Star, 36, 57, 92, 101
Washington Times, 57
Webster, H. T., 5
Welland, Dennis, 6
Wetterau, M. Rudolf, 96, 97, 105
white flannel suit, Mark Twain's, 36, 88–95
Whittier, John Greenleaf, 1, 14, 15
Wiener Luft, 5
Wiggin, Kate Douglas, 88
Wilde, Oscar, 12
Williams, True W., 7–8, 105
Wilson, David, 5, 61, 62, 105
Wing, Frank, 23, 52, 53, 105

Young, Art, 42, 105

Zola, Emile, 14, 15